# Table of Contents

# Introduction

First – congratulations on purchasing this book! I can only assume that you are serious about horseback riding and want to start out the right way. You'll hear me throughout this book talk about SAFETY, SAFETY, and SAFETY! You can never be too safe while being around these huge animals! We'll discuss the safety issue in depth at different points in the book.

I know you must have lots of questions – that's why have I prepared this book: To help anyone of any age to learn all the basics about horseback riding prior to getting on a horse for the first time. There are many things you need to understand before mounting and riding for the first time. This book will take you item by item through all of these critical concepts to help you understand how a horse thinks, how he's made, his physical characteristics, etc. You will also have to prepare yourself both physically and mentally.

Riding horses is like no other sport. If you play golf, tennis, swim, jog, play football or basketball, lift weights.... whatever it is (except for some team interaction) how well you do in that sport is pretty much determined by what YOU can do physically. How much speed, strength, finesse, coordination, etc. you can develop determines how well you'll do. But, when riding, you now have a partner — the horse — who, unlike a tennis racquet or golf club — has a mind of his own. Success depends on you working together as a team. Plus, your physical build and shape will also determine how well your horse can perform. Together you are a team and you can help each other out by being physically fit. Horseback riding also helps you develop specific muscle groups that are not worked regularly in other sports.

In the horse world, your success is determined by how well you can control, understand and harmonize with a 1.000-pound animal that has superior strength, is faster and has a better-developed nervous system than you. The way you overcome these strengths in a horse is to understand what the horse's limitations are.

Understanding the horse's body, what makes him tick and how the horse's brain works is the key to controlling him. If you don't figure this out

# Chapter 1: Horse Basics – A Quick Overview

## Understanding the Mind of a Horse

Of all the things to learn and understand that will help you get ready to handle and control horses, the most important is understanding how he thinks. The horse's brain is not like the brain of a human. You must understand that a horse cannot reason like humans and almost all training is a series of controlled actions that became habits. You and I can take in multiple senses, deduce and figure things out and actually plan for things and react in a reasoned way. Horses do not have this capacity – and the quicker you can understand this one concept the much easier it will be for you to know how to handle a horse and realize why he reacts the way he does to different things around him.

Next, as a rider you must understand the whole history of the horse is one as a **prey animal.** He is not a predator. That is, horses do not go after other animals to kill them or eat them. The horse's first reaction to anything he is unsure of is "**flight or fight**." Most horses choose flight; however, there are some that will choose to fight. Whether it is that is challenging him, perhaps a predator, or something simpler he doesn't understand, like a loud noise or a newspaper blowing in the wind – **he will almost always shy or flee from the thing he doesn't trust or understand.** Again, understanding that this reaction is normal helps you out as a horse handler and trainer. Keep in mind that many predators over the years saw the horse as part of the food chain. Even today, mountain lions, wolves, grizzly bears and other animals will threat and attack a horse if the situation is right. For that reason, the horse, understanding his position in the food chain, will run away once he realizes he is about to be under attack. He will flee first and ask questions later.

It is almost comical to see what a 1,000 pound horse will spook from at times: A simple noise, a paper blowing around, even a flag or something blowing in the wind. To them, when they don't understand it, they are all hose-eating boogey men. As a rider you must also understand that you are going to be sitting in the most vulnerable area of a horse – his back. If you have ever watched the Discovery channel and seen the zebras fleeing from the lions, then you know that the lion will almost always jump at the zebra's back. The same is true for horses and their predators. As a rider you are going to be on their back and at times this makes some horses very nervous.

This is something that you must be aware of at all times. You must avoid making any movements or doing anything that will make a horse fear you on his back.

Finally, **horses are herd animals.** That is, they desire to be with other horses or at least a trusted owner or trainer. Over the centuries they have found safety in numbers. While in a herd, one of the individual horses is less likely to be selected as a predator's meal. And, with many of them in the herd, the likelihood of one seeing an approaching predator is much greater since there are that many more eyes, ears and noses checking for potential danger.

That doesn't mean that all horses always get along. In fact, you'll immediately see how horses have their own pecking order within the herd. One will always emerge as a leader (what horse people often refer to as "alpha"). Some horses are naturally more dominant than others. There are also horses that seem to be loners. Because the horse no longer wanders the range, he has grown accustomed to living alone, although, many horses will appreciate having other equine friends nearby.

Now, when you insert a human into the life of a horse, this instinct to follow a leader is very helpful. If you can instill your leadership over a horse right away, then he'll follow you and you will be able to train and lead him whichever way you want. **You must gain the horse's respect early on.** If you don't, the horse will take charge and you will constantly be battling the horse for control.

If you had a bad experience with a horse and now you need to take control, there are methods to do so in advanced horse training. So all is not lost if something in the past has left the horse out of your control. If you desire to learn more about horse training methods, how to take control, teach a horse submission and fix the behavior problems, then you can go to www.HorseTrainingResources.com and see the excellent horse training materials available.

## *Understanding Horse Senses*

You really cannot equate the senses of a horse with that of a human. Remember, horses are prey animals but humans are predators. The senses each uses, while similar, are used in a much different ways and processed differently in the brain.

Let's take each sense and do a quick overview:

## Sight

Probably the most important sense a horse has is his sight. Given that he is a prey animal, as a horse in the wild, he will very much depend on his sight to see trouble coming that could mean the difference between life and death for him.

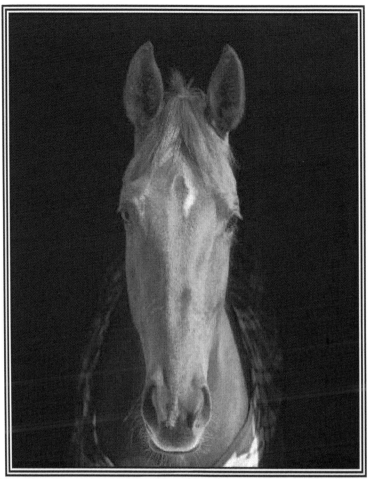

Horse's eyes are on either side of his long, narrow head. Horses have panoramic vision. They can see nearly 180 degrees on each side but they do have a blind spot directly behind them and directly in front of them. Their forward field of vision is binocular, which means they can see directly in front of them until about one foot in front of their head. This means that they cannot even see the food in their feeding bins!

It is also very important to remember that you should never approach a horse from behind. Unless he has his head turned and sees you, you could easily spook him and get kicked or force the horse to bolt forward. Approach a horse from the front or side, and if you must go behind him, keep a hand on him and let him know where you are at all times. As you walk behind a horse you should drag your hand along his back and hindquarters. Do not walk way out behind them, but rather walk directly behind them as close as you can. A horse needs leverage and reach to kick you. You are much safer when you walk directly behind versus way out behind. A kick close up will do less damage because the horse cannot get the momentum he needs to hurt you. If you are behind the horse but not out of striking distance you are more likely to break a bone due to the force and momentum the horse builds in a kick.

It is believed that horses can see for hundreds of yards and can differentiate colors somewhat. The horse's night vision is quite a bit better than humans – proven by many a story of those riding at night where the horse could see where they were going when the rider could not.

## Hearing

Horses can hear much better than humans. Something you might expect from a prey animal that survives by getting away from predators. Look at the shape of a horse's ear and you'll see it is similar to a funnel or cone. The horse has the ability to use its ears to channel sound to the ear canal very well.

Also notice that horses can move their ears quite a bit forward and to the rear and swivel them independently. They can also process sounds from each ear separately unlike humans. Their brains are programmed to take in each sound while the horse is eating or standing and determine if he should be alerted when he hears a sound from any direction.

You must be aware that horses will react quickly and be spooked by loud noises such as car horns, loud bangs, and even low flying planes. You can generally gentle the horse and settle him down to reassure him that it is okay. It is also important to remember that a horse will spook based on his rider. If a sound scares you and you jump in the saddle then you are also going to see a reaction from the horse. The sudden tensing in your body will alert him and he may jump sideways, stop suddenly or speed up.

## Smell

Horses have a very well developed sense of smell – much more sensitive than a human. They can smell other animals in the area and be alerted to things quite quickly when they get a whiff from being downwind.

The sense of smell is also used to check out or size up other horses. You'll notice that they always approach, both other horses and humans, with their nose. It is their way of determining if they are friendly or not.

Always approach a horse that doesn't know you with the back of your hand extended in a slow gesture. The horse will sniff your hand to determine if you're safe to be around or not. This process is putting the horse at ease about you. Without doing that he'll generally just flee because he can't trust you and he's the prey animal.

## Touch

Horses have a fairly thick hide but not like you might think. They can feel things as light as a fly on their skin so it must not be too thick!

The horse has well formed nerve endings that can feel even light touches from his friends and humans alike. Watch as horses interact and touch each other with their muzzles and rub up against each other.

You can use the sense of touch to your advantage around a horse by gently rubbing it, patting them on the shoulder, and massaging them in special places. They love to be rubbed on their faces – up between the eyes. Many horses enjoy being rubbed up around the ears. But you must do this gently and slowly. After a while, a horse will become accustomed to your rubbing and will start to lower their heads with contentment. This is a clear sign that the horse trusts you and is at ease with your actions. Many professional trainers will tell you that you must be able to rub a horse all over the body in order to earn his complete trust. This is an excellent concept to practice when you groom your horse on a daily basis. Grooming is very relaxing for a horse and allows you to find all his ticklish spots.

## How to 'Read' A Horse – Body Language

Horses use body language on a daily basis. They are also keen to pick up your body language as well. Horses are highly social creatures and they talk to each other in various ways. As humans, we must be able to read the basic body language that the horse exhibits. As children, one of the first body language signs that we learn about are the facial gestures that a horse makes. If you were ever around ponies at pony rides or other horses, your parents probably told you that an angry horse lays their ears back. Ears that are laid back may also be accompanied by teeth barring, depending on how agitated the horse is. Some horses are just naturally grumpy and tend to leave their ears back all the time, no matter what you are doing with them.

There are several other facial expressions that you must take into consideration as a horse owner as well.

- **Fear:** A horse that is afraid of something usually has both ears pointing in that direction. He may also stand square and with his head high in the air, just before he takes off running. You may also be able to see the whites of the eyes and the tensing neck muscles. His nostrils may flare too.

- **Alert:** Many horses will stand square, heads held high and ears pointed straight forward. The horse may not be scared, but perfectly content with his surroundings. You will often see horses doing this when they hear another horse coming.

- **Threatening or Aggression:** This is the ear laid back, not happy look of a horse. These horses are often planning their next move if you agitate them any more. This may be one that involves teeth or hooves.

- **Relaxed:** A relaxed horse will just appear relaxed. His head will be at a medium to low height, his eyelids will be droopy and his ears will be relaxed (sometimes pointing to the side). His lower lip may be loose and he might be chewing softly or yawning. This is the expression you will normally see when they are being groomed or dosing off for a mid-afternoon nap.

Each horse will have a subtle variation of these gestures. Spending a lot of time with and around your horse will allow you to see his version of the gestures. You can also get a good view of these gestures if you spend time around a herd of horses at pasture. They will threaten each other if one gets to close, they will be alert at the sound of horses from another pasture, and they will take relaxing naps in the summer sun.

Equine body language can also be vocal. You will hear these sounds every morning when you go to feed. You know that piercing whinny from the barn that says, "I'm hungry! Come feed me!" Horses have a fairly small vocal range but each sound has a distinct meaning that many horse owners will learn very quickly.

- **Whinnying:** Used by a horse to announce his presence. The sound is designed to carry over long distances, that is why you hear it so well across a large pasture at feeding time. It's kind of like your horse saying, "Hey! Don't forget about me!" They can also use it as a complaint of loneliness or a "Wait for me!" call. Wild horses would use the gesture as a means of keeping in contact with the rest of the herd when they move out of sight.

- **Nickering:** Nickering can be equated to that of a cat's purr. The nicker is a deep, nasal sound that a horse makes with his mouth closed. Mares will often nicker to their foals. This sound is also used as a greeting to owners and other horses (especially if you have treats!). The sound is kind and friendly.

- **Blowing:** A horse can use a blow in several different ways. The first is that similar to a sigh in humans. They may blow when they are becoming impatient or when you are making him do something he doesn't really want to do. They can also use a blow as a warning. If a horse is curious about something, such as a new stable blanket, they may blow, wait and then investigate the new item. Some horses also blow when working, and in that situation, it's usually a sign of relaxation.

- **Snorting:** A snort is a harsh blow. Horses often snort in disapproval and at other horses. There can be a strong hint of aggression in a snort.

- **Squealing:** Squeals always sound worse than they really are. Stallions will squeal at new mares or teasing mares. Two stallions will often squeal at each other. The squeal is commonly used as an assertion of seniority. It is kind of like saying, "Hey, I was here first." The horse will usually hold his head high and ears forward. Mares in season sometimes squeal when being sniffed by a curious gelding. There are usually no real signs of aggression, although the noise itself sounds very aggressive.

## Range of Motion and Dangerous Moves

You must understand that horses can move with amazing speed, with great force and are always to be considered dangerous. They can turn their head and reach around to bite flies off their flanks and their legs can move much more quickly than you might think. Not only can the rear legs strike backwards with tremendous force, but the same rear leg can come forward and he can scratch their ears with their rear hooves.

Look at how large and strong the horses head, neck and shoulders are and look at the muscles they have. A simple head jerk or swinging around can easily knock you down.

Horses can pivot or swing left or right very quickly. If you are on his side and he decides to turn and move or flee, the force of his whole body will be swinging into you and you are no match to stop it. Remember this as you try to put a blanket or a saddle on a horse and he's spooked by it. If the front of the horse is swinging left then the back of the horse will be swinging right at the same time.

Horses can also side step quickly. If something spooks him on one side he'll move to the other side.

And, as you might expect, a horse can move forward and backward very quickly. If you approach him from the rear he might possibly either kick you or bolt forward. However, if you approach him from the front, say carrying something that he's concerned or spooked by; he may either back up quickly or rear. If you are holding onto a lead rope, don't try to stop this quick movement backward by force. This will excite him even more – and many horses had actually gone ballistic, even going over backward, trying to get away. There are many horses that are not accustomed to the pressure that is placed on a halter when they move suddenly in this manner. The pressure of you pulling on the rope will only make him fight it more. Even those horses that have been trained to give to pressure may revert to natural instinct and fight the pressure versus give to the pressure. This has led many horses falling on their backs.

## The Horse's Instinct Is to Flee

As you now know, and will definitely hear it again, a horse's first instinct will be to flee. If you make loud noises or sudden moves, if you are shaking out a blanket, or even coiling a rope – the horse may react by trying to get away. You should never make quick movements around a horse that doesn't know you or that hasn't had time to get used to you.

Your goal should always be to calm the horse, speak softly to him and cuddle him by rubbing him while you are in his presence or working around or on him. If you are introducing something new to the horse allow him to check it out on his own terms. If you have a new saddle pad and he isn't sure about, allow him to sniff and nibble on it. Then gently approach him with the blanket and rub it on his shoulder. If you are unsure as to how the horse will react to the new item, take the horse to a round pen or corral when introducing the horse to the item. This allows him more space if he feels he needs to get away from it. A cramped stall may not be enough room for him to get away and you may end up getting hurt.

# Chapter 2: Horse Anatomy

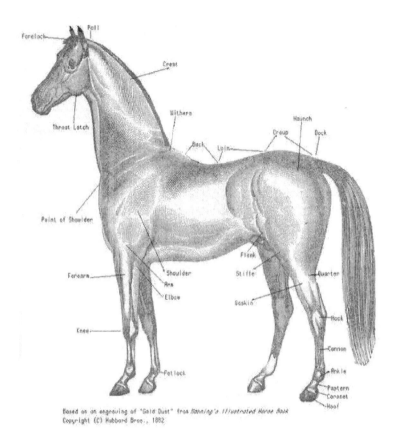

Based on an engraving of "Gold Dust" from *Manning's Illustrated Horse Book*
Copyright (C) Hubbard Bros., 1882

## Anatomy of the Horse

As a horse owner it is important to know many of the parts of the horse. If the horse were to get injured, you would need to be able to tell the veterinarian exactly which part of the horse was injured and you should be able to use the proper terms. While riding, it is also important to know several parts of the horse so that you can take instruction from a riding instructor, a trainer and even a book.

The important parts of the head include the poll, throatlatch and mouth.

- The **poll** is the area between the ears. This area is extremely sensitive and if hit hard enough could kill a horse. You should always be careful with a horse's poll. Never hit the horse between the ears with anything, including riding crops. Many "old school" trainers believed you could break a horse by hitting them between the ears with a riding crop; many horses have died from just that. Think of it as the soft spot on a baby's head.

- The **throatlatch** is the connection between the horse's head and neck. This is where the throatlatch of your bridle buckles.

- The **mouth** has several parts of its own that you can learn, but the most important area is the space without teeth. This is area is known as the bars of the mouth and is where the bit will rest.

Moving down the horse you have the neck. The top part of the neck is the **crest**. Some horses have very large crests, and it is usually most identifiable in stallions and some broodmares.

At the base of the neck are the **withers.** This area can be prominent in some horses and breeds, such as the Thoroughbred. However, each horse in every breed differs. The withers are important when it comes to fitting your horse with a saddle. The saddle pad and saddle will rest on the withers. Quarter Horses and Paint Horses have been noted for having small, but wide withers. Old horses will generally have prominent withers due to the arch in their aging backs.

While looking at the horse, it is obvious that the back is the place between the withers and the **loins.** You can find your horse's loins by moving straight up the area called the **flanks.** The flanks are the area where the horse's belly, or **barrel,** connects to the **hindquarters.** The loins are the area where there are no ribs. Down from the loins you have the hindquarters or the horse's rear end. It is important to note that the flanks are often sensitive in horses, especially males. The croup is the high point of the hindquarters. On some horses, it looks like a bump, and the area extends to the base of the tail, called the dock.

Moving down the horse's hind legs, on the front, you have the sensitive area of the flank and then the joint is called the **stifle.** Moving down the back of the hind leg, you have an area that sort of juts out. This is called the **hock.** Moving down some more you have the **cannon, ankle,** and **pastern.**

On the front legs you have the **shoulder** at the top connecting the leg and then the **forearm.** As you move down you have the **knee, cannon** again on the front and then the **fetlock.**

Around the top of each hoof you have an area that is somewhat white and scaly known as the **coronet**. This area is where the hoof actually grows out of the leg.

These are the most common parts of a horse that you will need to know as a horse owner and rider. These parts are important because you will use them to identify whether or not a horse has good conformation.

Conformation is the way that a horse is built. A horse with good conformation will often just look right. There are several conformation faults that you should be aware of before purchasing a horse.

**Ewe Neck**: This is a horse with a thin and oddly shaped neck. It often appears to be arched and abnormally thin at the top toward the head.

**Bull Neck:** This horse will appear to have an abnormally large neck that blends directly to the shoulder without any sort of junction. An actual bull often has a neck similar to this, hence the name. The bull neck should not be confused with the large crest that is conformational correct in baroque breeds like the Lipizzaner or Andalusian.

**Forelegs:** The forelegs have several flaws. The toes can be turned out or turned in. The feet can be too close together at a narrow base, sort of like the horse is bowlegged. The feet can also be spread far apart with the knees too close together, sort of like a knock-kneed person.

**Hind Legs:** Like the front legs, the hind legs also have similar conformational defects. These are most noticeable in the hocks.

**Pasterns:** Improper pasterns can lead to a number of soundness problems. A horse with upright pasterns moves as if he is digging into the ground, while a horse with long pasterns can move as if he is slapping the ground with his feet. Draft horses are often noted for having short, upright pasterns because they need the leverage for pulling. Thoroughbreds are often known to have longer pasterns.

# Chapter 3: Riding Styles & Tack

When you begin with the riding, you can choose one of the several different riding styles. Each discipline has its own style and competitive events associated with it. When choosing a riding style you are going to want to consider what it is that you really want to do with your horse as well as what your horse is capable of doing.

If you just want to spend the weekends on the trail, then you are probably going to find that a nice and cushioned western saddle is just what you need. If you want to learn to jump, then you are going to need to learn to ride English and use an English saddle. You may also choose a particular discipline because of what is popular in your area because of the availability of instructors and shows. Some styles are more popular in different areas of the country such as English riding (hunter/jumper or dressage) in the Northeast or Western riding in the West.

## Western

Many people enjoy the comfort and security that the western saddle provides. These saddles are large, cushiony and well suited for long rides. They were designed by cowboys who spent long hours and many days on horseback. They needed comfort on the trail and would even use them as pillows at night.

There are several variations of the western saddle as it has been adapted for specific events. There are saddles that are designed specifically for pleasure, trail, roping, cutting, barrel racing and reining. Each saddle may have unique features depending on what they are designed for. A cutting saddle is going to have a deep seat and large cantles to hold you in place while the horse makes quick maneuvers. The roping saddle is going to have a large horn for dallying your rope on. The barrel saddle is light with less skirting. They may also have taller cantles and a smaller horn. If you just plan on riding western for the fun of it, then you are most likely going to choose a pleasure or trail saddle.

If you are interested in riding western you will find that many cowhands who still work cattle are still using the western saddle. The western saddle is a large part of the cowboy heritage and it is not going away any time soon. The biggest function of the western saddle today, however, is going to be seen in use on pleasure horses and western show horses. There are several events that you can take part in while riding western including rodeos, western pleasure, trail riding (both for pleasure and competition), reining, roping, cutting and gymkhana. Those riders who ride for the sheer fun of riding are often seen in a comfortable western saddle.

Horses you might commonly see in Western tack include the Quarter Horse, although that breed has made a cross into English and dressage. The Paint and Appaloosas are also largely western breeds as well. You don't often see a Thoroughbred in a western saddle, but there are several out there who do work in a western saddle. Some gaited horses are often ridden western such as the Missouri Fox Trotter and the Tennessee Walking Horse. Arabians are often shown western as well, and special western saddles have been developed for their shorter backs and lighter bodies.

## *English*

The English saddle is much smaller and lighter than the western saddle. The style of English riding is often referred to as Hunt Seat, which refers back to the traditional foxhunts that take place in Britain. The English saddle is rather simple with stirrup leathers and metal stirrups.

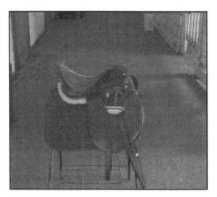

This saddle does not provide the security that the western saddle provides and the rider must rely on her balance more so than in a Western saddle. The rider also has closer contact with the horse and is easily able to feel the movements of the horse's shoulders and body. English saddles include different types, which vary somewhat in seat depth, narrowness of the twist of the saddle, and flap placement, such as hunt seat saddle, jumper saddle, dressage saddle and general purpose saddle. The stirrup leathers are easily adjustable so that the rider is able to adjust the length and distribute their weight properly while mounted. This is important because the English rider uses shorter stirrups than the western rider will, especially if jumping. A general-purpose saddle can be used in most English events including jumping and occasionally dressage, though most experienced riders find that the "all purpose" isn't specific enough in design to either discipline to make a proper advanced rider saddle.

Some English saddles include:

- **Dressage:** These saddles will have longer side panels and the rider will use a long stirrup, similar to that of a western rider. The longer stirrup length allows them to achieve the deep seat necessary for classical dressage riding. Dressage saddles are traditionally black.

- **Show Jumping:** These saddles are somewhat smaller than the general-purpose saddle and tend to have more padding in the knee rolls. This allows more support for the rider's legs while the horse is in a jumping motion. Some show jumping saddles have a more pronounced rise through the seat as it leads to the cantle, causing the rider to sit more forward.

- **Hunt Seat:** The hunt seat saddle is a flat English saddle, traditionally with little depth to the seat. (A show jumping saddle may be slightly deeper in the seat to give the rider more security.) The hunt seat saddle is often used in the hunt seat equitation competition, so it will traditionally lack knee flaps (or have small knee padding).

- **Saddle Seat:** These saddles are flatter in the seat and have slightly longer panels similar to that of a dressage saddle. However, the panels are much wider and thin. These saddles are seen in use on gaited horses.

## Bridles and Bits

For each discipline there is a specific type of bridle and bit to be used. The bridle and the bit are the primary means of communication between you and your horse. The bridle holds the bit in place and the bit encourages the horse to adopt the correct head carriage. "Signals" are sent to the horse through the bit and bridle by specific pressure points on the lips, tongue and nose.

There are several different styles of bridles, but you will find that there are both English and western bridles. Western bridles typically consist of a simple leather headstall. It may or may not have brow bands or throatlatches. Many may also have simple leather loops that fit around the horse's ear. The traditional western bit is the "curb bit", however, many young horses are first ridden in snaffle bits. A curb chain is present if the horse is using a curb bit. The curb has long shanks to which the reins attach. There are also several fancy western bridles that feature silver and beading for the show ring. These will also vary in style and design.

The English bridle also has a few variations to match the variations found in the saddles. The bridle is typically a single rein that attaches to a simple snaffle bit. The bridle will have a browband, throatlatch and cavesson. The cavesson goes around the bridge of the nose and is also known as the noseband. The dressage bridle and saddle seat bridle is a variation of the hunt seat bridle. Dressage bridles are typically black and sometimes with white piping over the browband and noseband. For lower levels of dressage, the snaffle bridle is used, sometimes with a flash or dropped noseband. For upper levels of dressage, a double bridle is used.

Bits are made out of various different types of metals. Some of the best bits were made from aluminum, but they are very hard to find these days. These bits were extremely light bits that a horse would easily carry in their mouths. Many bits today are made from steel and copper. Copper is inlaid to the mouthpieces as they are sweet and encourage the horse to lick, salivate and keep a soft mouth. When choosing a bit you need to determine the level of your horse's training. If you purchased the horse fully trained, then the owner most likely told you what type of bit they used while riding the horse and you should have seen it when you test rode the horse.

One of the safest and most popular bits is the snaffle bit. The snaffle bit is very simple and uses direct contact to turn the horse. The snaffle bit features a jointed straight bar with large rings on both ends to which the reins and cheek pieces attach. There are variations on the rings as they can be O-ring, Egg-butt rings or D-rings. The mouthpiece itself has variations such as wire and twisted mouthpieces, but they are more severe. Many of today's

Olympic horses still compete in a simple snaffle bit. The bit is considered the gentlest bit available.

The double bridle is a unique bridle that is often used by dressage and saddle seat riders. This is an English-type bridle that consists of a curb and snaffle bit. The snaffle is often called a bridoon in this bridle. These bridles are often seen on gaited horses. The snaffle bit causes the horse to raise the head while the curb causes the horse to maintain flexion at the poll and to yield with the lower jaw. The bridle gives the horse an appearance of having collection and a tucked head. This bridle is also used with two sets of reins.

The pelham bit is also a combination snaffle and curb bit. This bit is often used in hunters where the rider needs a little more control from the curb chain. This bit is used with two sets of reins and a curb chain. There are also a variety of rings available on these bits and the mouthpiece is often a plain, straight bar. This bit is commonly used in polo, hunting and jumping.

The curb bit is a single-bar mouthpiece that has a half-moon port in the center. There are variations on this bit with different port heights available. Most breed associations have various rules regulating the port height in horse shows. The port discourages the horse from slipping his tongue over the bit. The curb bit uses leverage on the bars of the mouth, versus the use of direct pull that is used with a snaffle. The bit is also available with a jointed mouthpiece. Although the jointed mouthpiece is similar to that of a snaffle bit, the bit is used in the same manner as a curb bit. These bits are often referred to as Cowboy Snaffles or Tom Thumb bits. The bit is used in conjunction with a curb chain or curb strap that goes behind the horse's chin. This strap tightens as the reins are pulled back.

Hackamores are devices that allow you to ride and control a horse without anything in his mouth. There are both English and Western versions of the hackamore. These are mechanical in nature and include metal shanks and some sort of protected metal loop that goes over the bridge of the nose. The English hackamore is similar but uses a leather strap over the nose. These bridles are not allowed in competition, although some jumpers are allowed to use them depending on association rules. The western bosal is also sometimes called a hackamore because it works in the same manner. This bridle consists of a rawhide loop that goes around the nose of the horse and the rider uses rope-type reins to control the horse.

Show competition rules may dictate what bits you may use in classes. Dressage shows are very particular about the use of bits approved by the United States Dressage Federation.

## Fitting a Saddle

Your horse won't want to go very far if the saddle doesn't fit properly. Many horses are sore in their backs and may try to avoid allowing you to ride all together if the saddle has been pinching them for quite some time. An unbalanced saddle will also cause the rider to ride unbalanced, which can affect the natural gait of the horse as it compensates for your lack of balance.

The saddle should fit without pinching, rocking or creating pressure points. If a horse has bald spots around the base of the withers, it usually means that the saddle is rubbing in those areas. The tree of the saddle must be the correct width and shape for the horse's back. A saddle that is too wide will sit low on the withers and create pressure points on the top of the withers. A saddle that is too narrow will pinch at the base of the withers and rub the hair off. A narrow saddle will also ride high in the front and cause the rider to be thrown back. This can also create pressure points on the back of the saddle. The saddle should be balanced so that the rider is able to maintain his balance without being thrown in any direction. The lowest part of the seat should be in the middle of the saddle. Many tack stores will allow you to try and test ride saddles to ensure that they fit your horse before you commit to buying them. Quarter Horses are known for needing wide treed saddles, while Thoroughbred type horses are known for needing narrow treed saddles. Each horse within a breed will vary, however.

The saddle must fit you as well. It is much easier to fit the saddle to the rider than it is to fit the saddle to the horse. The best thing to do is try out several saddles in the tack store before you go try it out on your horse. Most saddles are measured by their seat in inches, but to know which "size" you are, you will need to try several out at the tack shop.

Check the saddle fit on your horse by placing it on the horse's back without a saddle pad. The part of the saddle should touch the horse's spine, whether it is English or Western. You should also be able to fit two fingers between the saddle and the withers when the rider is mounted. Run your hand over the back of the horse's shoulder blade and under the front of the saddle. The saddle should not pinch or dig into these areas. This will allow the horse ample room for the spine and movement in the shoulders.

A saddle pad is often necessary for the comfort of the horse. There are various saddle pads for the type of saddle that you purchase. The saddle pad provides cushion between the saddle and your horse's back. This cushion allows for your weight to be evenly distributed along the back of the horse. This aids the horse in carrying your weight. You may also unbalance a horse if you use too much cushion.

# Chapter 4: Preparing for Your Ride

There are several preparatory steps you must take before you go saddling and bridling your horse. These steps are very important in ensuring that you and your horse will have a comfortable ride. Horses are not always ready to go when you are and you will need to prepare him properly for the ride.

## *Grooming*

Grooming is not only essential before riding, but if you are able to do it on a daily basis your horse will benefit greatly. Many people consider grooming as just cleaning up a horse, but in actuality you are doing much more than that for your horse. As you groom the horse you are getting his circulation going. You are also providing your horse with some much-needed human contact. Horses that are not touched on a regular basis will tend to revert back to the idea that they don't want to be touched. By grooming on a regular basis your horse is bonding with you and learning to trust you. This makes him a much easier friend to be around and safer to handle.

You should always groom your horse before riding. We do this, not only for cleanliness reasons, but to ensure that the hair is lying in the proper directions. By grooming you are removing any debris that may cause irritation between the horse's body and the tack he is going to be wearing. Pieces of hay, straw, dirt and burrs will poke into the back of the horse if he is not groomed prior to riding. If a burr were to suddenly stick the horse in the back while you were riding, you may find yourself going one way and the horse going the other. The most important aspect of the pre-ride groom is picking out the horse's feet. If the horse has shoes, you will need to remove any dirt and rocks that may be packed between the hoof and the shoe. Not removing this debris may cause the shoe to become loose or the hoof to become bruised. You will also want to remove any mud that is packed into the cavity of the hoof. This makes for a comfortable ride for the both of you.

You will need a few supplies to groom a horse properly. It is always nice to have a bucket or tote that you can keep your grooming supplies in and carry them wherever you need to. A bucket is required for bathing the horse as well.

## Basic Grooming Supplies:

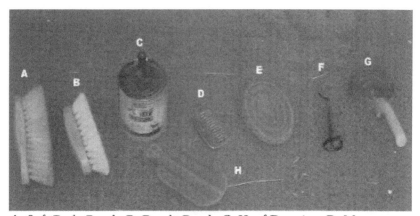

A. Soft Body Brush, B. Dandy Brush, C. Hoof Dressing, D. Mane Comb, E. Rubber Currycomb, F. Hoof Pick, G. Metal Currycomb, H. Plastic Bathing Brush

To begin grooming the horse, you will start with the rubber or metal currycomb. Rub the horse all over in a circular motion and loosen any dirt and dead hair. Follow behind the currycomb with the dandy brush. Do not use either the currycomb or the dandy brush on the horse's face. Use your metal currycomb to clean your dandy and soft brush as you go. Use the soft brush to remove dust and flatten out the hair. The soft brush may be gently used on the horse's face. Clean around the eyes and nostrils with a damp sponge or rag. Pick out the feet starting with the left front, left hind, right front and then right hind. Remove any rocks and dirt. Ensure that shoes are not loose for safe riding. Apply hoof dressing if the hooves appear to be dry.

Some horses may require this more than others and this will also depend on the weather in your area. If you live in a hot climate, the hooves tend to be drier and require more dressing.

## Wrapping Legs the Right Way

Many riders will use bell boots, shin splints or polo wraps to protect their horse's legs. If you ride western, you may use simple Velcro splint boots and possibly bell boots. Bell boots are used to protect the heel of the horse if they are known to interfere, or kick their heels with their hind legs. If you ride English, you will probably wrap the front legs or all four legs with polo wraps. If you are jumping or working in tight patterns your horse should have some leg protection.

If using polo wraps you must be careful when wrapping the legs, as improper wrapping can cause a horse to strain or bow tendons. This is due to improper force and stress placed on the tendons from the wrap. If you use Velcro boots, you need to ensure that the Velcro is straight across to prevent uneven tension as well.

Follow these steps when wrapping with polo wraps:

1. Begin at the top of the cannon bone, just below the knee or hock. Place the wrap on the outside of the leg to begin with.
2. Wrap down first by wrapping behind the tendons front to back. The wrap should be even and snug. Overlap each time by half to three-quarters of the width of the wrap. If you are on the left side of the horse, you will wrap in a counterclockwise direction and on the right side you will wrap clockwise.
3. When your wrap reaches the fetlock, cup the joint with the wrap and begin wrapping back up to the top.
4. Pay close attention to the width of the wrap as you are wrapping. You only want one wrap at the top of the cannon bone. If you have enough wrap to wrap all the way back down the leg, you will need to start over. It is important that the wrap is consistent on the lower part of the leg. The Velcro should also be straight across the leg and not angled.

Polo wraps should not be left on the horse for an extended period of time. They should be removed after every workout. Not all horses will need their hind legs wrapped unless they are doing work where they sit on their hindquarters, such as in a sliding stop or canter pirouette. For everyday riding, your horse will have sufficient protection with only the front legs wrapped.

## Longeing (or Lungeing)

If your horse has spent a lot of time locked up in his stall due to the weather, etc. then you will want to warm him up before you ride. These horses are typically very excited to get out and they will have a lot of energy to spend before they are ready to think properly for a ride. Longeing is one of the best ways to judge your horse's attitude for the day and determine if he will be safe to ride.

Most horses will buck for a little bit once you get them going. You will want to allow them to get their excitement out and then concentrate on putting them through their paces. Work on the basic gaits and in both directions. This will get the muscles warmed up and calm the horse down. If you have a small corral or round-pen you can longe the horse with or without a rope. You can also longe with or without tack.

When you are longeing you don't want to be chasing the horse around the pen. You will want him to follow the pressure of the longe line and you will want to drive him forward by standing behind his shoulder. Many horses are very sensitive to this. They will drive when you are behind the shoulder and they will stop when you step in front of it. You also want to be certain that his nose is tipped slightly toward you and that his eyes are focused on you. You do not want him to have his head away from you and looking for his buddies. This means that he is not paying attention to you at all.

When longeing you will want to direct the horse with the hand of the direction you are going. If you are going toward the left then the longe rope will be in your left hand and the excess will be in your right. The same is true when the horse is going to the right. You may also twirl the end of the excess rope to create more driving force. If the horse is not paying attention to you or stops, don't be afraid to give him a light pop on the rump with the rope.

Many horses will only want to go to the left. This only means that they have not been worked to the right enough or possibly not handled on the right hand side enough. (Thoroughbreds off the track have worked primarily going left (counter clockwise), so they are often stiff, unbalanced or resistant in working to the right.) It is important that we give adequate attention to both sides in our daily handling of the horse.

Some horses will just need patience and practice when learning to longe. Once they learn it, though, you will find that longeing is a technique that you can use in a variety of situations. If the horse begins to anticipate when you turn him, you will need to mix up your pattern. Begin turning him in different parts of the pen and at different times. This will keep him thinking.

Eventually, you may not even feel like you are driving the horse. The horse will begin to work around you and take commands as they are given. This is very nice to see and you will appreciate not having to constantly encourage the horse to go. After about ten to fifteen minutes of longeing, your horse should be limber enough and mentally prepared to ride. Remember that every horse is different and some may take longer than others, especially if they have been on a long winter lay-up. Give your horse a well-deserved rest before bridling and getting ready to mount.

You must keep in mind that longeing is hard on a horse's joints, so keep the longe time limited to 20 minutes at most, and try not to longe every day. Faster gaits on the longe are harder on the horse, so try to ensure that you warm him up at the walk for several minutes before asking him to trot.

## Saddling & Bridling

It is very important that the saddle is positioned correctly on the horse's back. Follow these steps for proper saddling.

1. Begin by placing the saddle pad on the horse's back slightly in front of the withers and then slide it back into the position. The pad should rest a few inches above the withers and at the base of the neck. This keeps the hair under the saddle pad smooth.

2. Next, place the saddle over the pad and pull the blanket up into the gullet of the saddle. This keeps the pad from tightening down on the withers. While you place the saddle on the horse, be certain that you do not flop the stirrups on the horse. On western saddles you will want to flip the right stirrup as well as the girth over the top of the saddle. On the English saddles you will want to slide the stirrups up to the top of the leathers. About 3 inches of pad should be visible at both the front and the back of the saddle for an English saddle. For the western saddle you will want about 3 inches of pad in the front, but you may have more in the back. You will know that the saddle is in the right position if the girth will fit perfectly behind the horse's elbow. A dressage saddle sits further back on a horse, and you'll know that the saddle is in position if the girth is a hand's width from the horse's elbow.

3. On the western saddle the girth is attached to the saddle on the right side. On the English saddle this is not necessarily the case. If you are riding English you will need to attach your girth to the right side of the saddle and then attach it on the left side of the saddle. On the western saddle, you will gently undrape the girth and stirrup from the top of the saddle. You will then reach under the horse on the left side and attach the girth.

4. When securing the girth on the English saddle you will do so gradually. Move up the holes slowly so as not to suddenly tighten the girth on the horse. If you run out of holes on the left side, move to the right side and

move it up from there. On a western saddle you will loop the latigo strap through the D-ring on the girth. Continue to loop until you have about a foot of latigo left and the needle on the D-ring fits into the hole. You will then place the excess in the latigo keeper. You may also tie a western cinch knot; however, many riders no longer use the knot for safety reasons. The knot can make it difficult to get the saddle off in an emergency situation.

5. Now, you will check your stirrup lengths. If you are the only one using the saddle, then there is a good chance that they are where they need to be. You can check your stirrup length by placing your hand under the flap above the stirrup leather. Using your left hand, place the stirrup against your outstretched arm. The stirrup should reach to your armpit. After mounting the horse, you will be able to determine whether or not the stirrups are at a comfortable length for you. On an English saddle the stirrups should rest at your ankle with your leg stretched downward. In a western saddle, you should be able to stand in the stirrups and maintain your balance for a few seconds.

The bridle should always be placed on the horse last because your horse must be tied during the saddling process. You should never tie a horse with the reins of a bridle. This is dangerous because if the horse were to pull back there would be damage to the horse's mouth as well as your tack. If you need to tie your horse while he is bridled, put his halter back on over the bridle, and then tie him by the halter. If you are tying him with your leadline, always use a slip knot, so that you can pull it to release in case of emergency. To tie a slip knot with your leadline, wrap the left and right pieces of the line around something, for example a fence post. Think of the left piece that goes up to the halter and the right piece goes to the end. Make a loop with the right piece and push it up under the wrapped left. Now pull the loop and the left piece tight so the loop sits snugly under the wrap. You'll have a small remainder that sticks out of the bottom, and this is the piece you pull to release the knot.

Before you begin to bridle the horse you first need to remove the halter and buckle it again around his neck. If you have an English bridle then you want to make sure that your throatlatch and noseband are unbuckled. If you have a western bridle, your throatlatch should be unbuckled if you have one.

1. Put the reins over the horse's head and lay them on the neck.
2. Stand at the left side of your horse and hold the bit in your left hand the top of the bridle with your right hand. Face forward in the direction of the horse and let the bit lie in your outstretched fingers.
3. Place your right hand, holding the top of the headstall, between the horse's ears.
4. Open the horse's mouth and insert the bit. You may need to stick your thumb in the corner of the mouth and rub the bars to get them to open the mouth.
5. Once the bit is in the mouth, gently slide the ears into the headstall. Pull the forelock out so that it is lying out of the browband.
6. Buckle the throatlatch and the noseband if you have one. The throatlatch should have about two fingers of space to ensure that the horse can breathe and flex at the poll. If you have a curb strap, ensure that it is not too tight and it should only make contact when the reins are pulled back.
7. Remove the halter from around the horse's neck.

# Chapter 5: Ready to Ride

Okay, so now your horse is warmed-up, he's tacked up and you're now ready for the moment you've been waiting for! However, let's consider a few things before we ride off into the sunset.

## Scared? Maybe just a little?

Those with little riding experience may have a certain amount of fear about riding a horse which is perfectly normal. A horse is one big animal after all and even some of the smaller ones can be intimidating to a new rider. This fear is perfectly normal and it's okay to be somewhat afraid, as long as you don't allow the fear to keep you from getting on the horse and trying it out. If you are uncertain, then you will want to be sure that your horse is a safe and steady mount and you may want to take a few riding lessons to get yourself comfortable and to ride in the presence of a professional.

## Being the Leader

Now, the next thing you need to keep in mind is that once you are in the saddle, you are supposed to be the leader. The key to being a successful rider is being a successful leader. A horse will not be willing to trust someone that doesn't exert their leadership. This begins on the ground, so if you're not a good leader on the ground then the horse isn't going to trust you much when you're in the saddle.

Horses are herd animals and they depend on a leader for their safety. If you get on with confidence and you are ready to go, then the horse is going to sense this and he is going to trust you. But when you get on a horse and you're uncertain about what to do, the horse will quickly assume the leadership role and tell *you* what *he* is going to do. It doesn't matter to the horse if you like it or not. You're just not somebody he can depend on yet.

To be confident and have this leadership concept down, you may want to consider riding lessons first. This will give you the opportunity to ride a horse that is accustomed to students and you will be able to build your confidence to a level that allows you to be the leader for your horse. This way, when you have your own horse and you go out to ride him, you will be the leader he is looking for.

## *Mounting*

Okay, so now it's the moment you've been waiting for. Mounting, believe it or not, is one of the hardest things about riding. Especially if you're not as flexible as you used to be. Kids seem to climb up without any trouble at all.

Mounting can be made easier on both you and the horse with a mounting block. Most English riders will use a mounting block because the English saddle is significantly harder to get into, but a mounting block in general relieves a lot of pressure that is put on a horse's back during the mounting process. You can use these every time to get on your horse if one is available. There may be times, however, when you will have to mount from the ground.

Begin by leading your horse to the area where you will be riding. If you are riding in an arena, lead the horse into the arena. Ensure that the ground is loose and dry. A wet arena is dangerous and you do not want to ride in one. Turn the horse so that he is facing the arena entrance while you are mounting. You don't want him facing away because he might be surprised by the sound of someone coming into the arena. Now, place the reins over the horse's head and rest them on his neck while keeping them in the left hand. Stand at the left shoulder of the horse, facing the rear. With your right hand, turn your stirrup as needed and insert your left foot. Be careful that you do not poke the horse with your toe. Now, be super graceful, bounce a couple of times and launch yourself up. At the same time you want to swing your right leg over the horse, being careful not to kick him and then gently lower yourself into the saddle. Insert your right foot into the stirrup and take up your reins in the proper position for riding.

If you have a friend with you, when mounting from the ground, it is better for the horse's back to have someone holding down the right stirrup while you mount. This also helps to keep the saddle from shifting to the left as you mount.

Mounting with grace is difficult and comes along with practice. Don't worry if you feel silly while you are mounting as it is quite a difficult thing to master the first few times. A well-trained horse should not move while you are mounting.  He should stand still and wait for your cue to move.  Some horses, however, have picked up these bad habits so do not be alarmed if the horse takes a few steps.  In some cases, a horse will take a step to adjust to your weight on his body.  If, while mounting from the ground, you have correctly faced the rear of the horse, if your horse takes a few steps, you will still be able to keep up with him; whereas, if you were facing the side or front of the horse, and your horse walks a step or two while you are mounting, you may find yourself hopping to try to catch up.

## Holding the Reins & Rein Cues

Depending on the discipline you chose, you have two options when it comes to holding your reins. An English rider holds the reins in both hands, taking up enough reins to have contact with the horse's mouth. This will leave some slack in the reins between their hands. The western rider will usually hold the reins together in their left hand only, if the horse is wearing a curb bit and if the horse knows how to neck-rein. If the horse is wearing a regular snaffle bit, then the western rider can hold the reins in a manner similar to that of an English rider.

There are several different types of rein cues. The hands and the reins work together to form the natural aid of the hands. The reins are simply an extension of the hands. And the hands complement the legs.

Here are the different rein cues that you can use:

**Direct Rein:** This rein cue maintains straightness in the horse without allowing it to bend left or right. The hand pulls the rein directly back toward the rider's hip.

**Indirect Rein:** Bends the horse to either the right or the left. If you will use an indirect rein to turn right, then you will place the right hand above the withers and the left hand should move outward and forward to allow the horse to bend to the right. This is often used for controlling the haunches and lateral moves.

**Leading/Opening Rein:** This rein cue leads the horse in the direction you want to go. This is also known as an "open" rein. The rider extends her arm out to the side of the direction she wishes to turn the horse.

**Neck Rein:** Exerts pressure on one side of the horse's neck. Both hands move in the same direction to guide the horse. This rein aid is commonly used in western riding when using a curb bit and riding with one hand.

**Pulley Rein:** This is also known as an emergency rein. This rein uses extreme force in an upward and backward action to force the horse to stop. You only use one rein in an extreme emergency situation, such as a runaway. This maneuver will cause the horse to turn its head toward you and to circle.

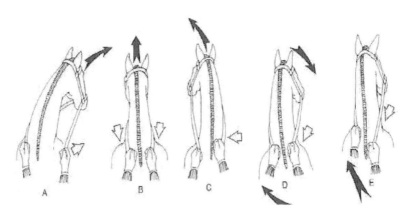

A. Leading or Opening Rein, B. The Direct Rein, C. The Neck Rein, D. The Indirect Rein in front of withers, E. The Indirect Rein behind the withers

## The Seat

The seat (also known as "weight") is an equally important aid to riding. Correct use of the seat aid assists in getting the horse to move forward or stop, in addition to turning. When you want to stop, you sink your weight into your seat into the saddle.

This tells your horse that you are preparing to stop and you are stopping your forward motion. This alerts him to the fact that he needs to stop his forward motion as well. The seat can be also be used to drive the horse forward by using a little push (think of using your seat to push a book across a table).

The seat should always follow the motion of your horse's hindquarters. To obtain this secure seat, you must be sitting in a saddle that allows you to do so. To find your seat, you can stop your horse, stand in your stirrups and then sit straight down. Then allow your weight to drop into your heels. A straight line should be formed from the ear through the shoulder through your hip joint and to the back of the heel. The lower back should be flat and the seat bones should be able to push downward and forward.

Many riders make the mistake of perching themselves forward in the saddle or rounding the shoulders and hunching over. This position also causes you to be ahead of the motion of the horse and will cause you to fall forward when the horse moves. To fix this seat, you should tighten your abdominals and rock the seat bones under the body, lift up from your sternum and breathe deeply into your belly.

Many new riders tend to sit in the saddle as if they are sitting in their recliner. In this position they are rolling their seat bones back against the cantle of the saddle. This causes them to raise their thighs and lower legs and causes them to be behind the motion. These riders need to sit up and lower their legs. To get the leg in the proper position, think of pushing your thigh and knee to the ground.

Your weight (also known as "seat") will adjust with every aid that you use. A sensitive horse will be able to pick up the changes in your weight before you even ask for the cue. Some horses are so sensitive that they will respond to just a rider's shift in weight, for example, when performing a leg yield and the rider shifts the weight into her seat bone of the direction in which she wishes to travel. Your weight will adjust as soon as you begin thinking about the cue you are going to give. As your weight adjusts, the horse naturally adjusts to stay under you.

Think of what it's like to carry a backpack. When it shifts on your back, you adjust by moving under it slightly. When your weight shifts, your horse adjusts to where you've shifted.

The rider should maintain a straight back and pelvis so they do not give incorrect weight cues to their horse. Tipping to either side will cause you to constrict the muscles in one side of your body, which may cause your horse to move at an angle. The shoulders should maintain in parallel position with the horse's shoulder.

## The Legs

There are two basic leg positions in riding. The first position is called *at the girth*. This is where the rider's calf is against the horse just behind the edge of the girth. This position is used to bend the horse and drive the horse forward. The second position is called *behind the girth*. This is about four inches behind the *at the girth* position.

Stirrups too long.

Stirrups too short.

Stirrups just right.

The legs are used to bend the horse through turns and to cue him to move forward. When you are going forward you squeeze with the thighs and wait for a response from the horse. If there is no response, you squeeze with the calves. At the same time you want your reins to be slack so that you are not giving any conflicting commands. If the horse does not respond to a squeeze from the calf, then you can gently kick with **one** foot. Don't go kicking and swinging your legs like a wild banshee.

To use your legs in turning you will apply pressure from the opposite leg that you are cueing the turn for. For example, if you are turning right, then you will pull (or squeeze) the right rein and give pressure with the left thigh. The same goes for the left turn. Pull with the left rein and give pressure with the right thigh. To bend your horse properly through the turn, you would apply pressure with the calf of the direction you are turning in. For example, when turning left, apply left calf pressure. While you are riding you want to maintain contact and you can gently squeeze to encourage the horse to go faster.

To use the legs properly the stirrups must be properly adjusted as well. If they are too long you will not be secure in your seat and you will not be able to use your leg properly. If they are too short, you will put a lot of pressure on your ankles and knees and may use too much leg in your cues.

## Voice

We often use our voices as a command. While longeing we will verbally tell our horses to walk, trot (or jog) and canter (or lope). We also use "whoa" when we want them to stop. Clucking and kissing are also voice commands that are commonly used. Clucking to your horse encourages the horse to move faster, such as into a trot or to increase his stride. When you kiss or smooch at a horse, you are often cueing him into a canter or lope. These are the two most common voice commands next to the "whoa."

Many instructors prefer riders not to use voice commands or audible cues like clucking because they become bad habits and are not allowed in the show ring. (Points will be deducted for verbal cues.) Riders also need to be sensitive to the fact that other horses around them can be quite reactive to clucking or kissing sounds.

## Artificial Aids

Some people may tell you that you need to use a riding crop or spurs on your horse. This is entirely up to you if you choose to do so. Some horses may need a little extra encouragement and artificial aids can be useful and effective when used properly. If you are a beginning rider, you will most likely want to avoid these items until you feel comfortable and in control with your natural aids. By introducing artificial aids you are just giving yourself something else to worry about.

The artificial aids are merely an extension of your natural aids. A crop or whip can be used as an extension of the arm and to strengthen leg cues. Spurs are meant to reinforce the leg aids as well. These aids should only be used if you are not strong enough to cue your horse naturally. Some horses are rather large and need that extra help to feel the aids properly.

These aids should not be used until you have had the chance to ride the horse and assess his responsiveness to your natural aids. If you feel that you are not strong enough to elicit the response that you desire, then you may consider using an artificial aid. For example, some horses cannot respond to the leg of a child because they are not strong enough. A riding crop can be used to reinforce their leg aids.

A rider who uses a spur for all leg cues will often find that his natural leg cues go ignored. This is because horses can become desensitized to the spur and the same is true for the riding crop. A desensitized horse will require harder and sharper jabs, and this can quickly become inhumane. This is why you must use such aids sparingly.

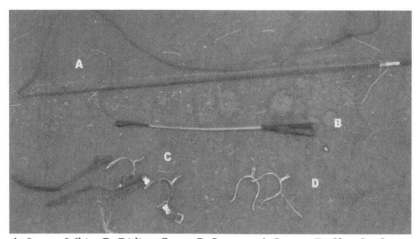

A. Lunge Whip, B. Riding Crop, C. Spurs with Straps, D. Slip-On Spurs

# Chapter 6: The Gaits

The gaits are the horse's natural way of moving. All horses have four natural gaits. These are the walk, the trot (or jog), the canter (or lope) and the gallop. Some horses are bred to have special gaits. These horses are called gaited horses and they are either trained to perform these gaits or they are natural to the horse. Some horses also have the innate tendency to pace rather than trot. South American breeds also have gaits that are unique to the breed.

The rider may influence the quality of a horse's gaits. Any gait may be performed poorly if the rider is riding poorly. Some horses can also be lazy and perform their gaits in a sloppy manner. An occasional accident or laziness is not usually enough to alter a horse's gait permanently, but if the mistake becomes a consistent habit then it may change the way that the horse moves. The horse's natural gaits are very efficient, but there can be irregularities that can cause them to be less efficient.

When riding, it is very important that you have a good understanding of the gaits and how to ride them. Here we will cover the basic gaits that you will ride.

## The Walk

The walk is a four-beat gait. As a horse walks, you will four distinct hoof beats as each foot strikes the ground. Two or three legs are always on the ground, which not only makes the walk the most stable gait but also the easiest to ride.

The sequence of the walk is:

- Left hind
- Left fore
- Right hind
- Right fore

When a horse begins to walk it may appear that the horse is moving with the front end first, but the power of the horse comes from the hindquarters and thus the walk sequence starts with the hind leg.

The four beats of the walk should be clear, distinct and evenly spaced. The horse should not shuffle or speed up and slow down through the gait. The walk should be a constant speed of about 4 miles per hour. When a horse is walking "pure" the horse should have a swinging back and good engagement. Each hind foot should also fall beyond the hoof print left by the front foot on the same side. While the horse walks he should also make generous relaxed balancing gestures with the head and neck with the tail swinging freely.

The walk may also have several faults. The gait has been called the easiest to ruin and the most difficult to repair. This is due to the fact that tension has developed as a result of forced training.

- *Jigging* is an irregular jog that a horse performs instead of walking. This is often difficult to control and uncomfortable to ride. A horse will often do this when he is anxious to catch up with other horses. Some horses seem to do this constantly and won't calm down into a nice walk.

- The *lazy walk* is a slow and toe-dragging walk. The gait lacks engagement, balance and a forward swing.

## The Trot

The trot is a two-beat diagonal gait. A diagonal gait is where the diagonal pairs of feet strike the ground together for one hoof beat and then the horse pushes off and is suspended in the air for a moment before the opposite diagonal pair of feet strike for the second beat.

The sequence of the trot is:

- Right hind and Left fore (suspension)
- Left hind and Right fore (suspension)

The moment of suspension is what gives the trot its bouncy feeling. The horse should not include any extra beats, shuffling or having a loss of suspension. The diagonal legs should move together and a good trot should have engagement from the hindquarters. The moment of suspension is longer when the trot is extended and the moment of suspension should be shorter in the collected or shortened trot. The tempo should remain the same regardless of whether or not the horse lengthens or shortens his stride. The speed of the normal trot should average between 6 and 8 miles per hour. A racing Standard bred may reach up to 30 miles per hour.

The *jog* is a relaxed, shortened trot with minimum suspension. This is usually seen in western horse competition. The gait is comfortable for both horse and rider over long distances.

As with the walk, a trot can also have many faults. The trot can be stiff and hollow, which causes the back muscles to tense and the horse is unable to have its natural swinging motion. This causes a rough trot that is difficult to ride. The trot can also have a loss of suspension, which causes the horse to lose its spring and suspension. This is usually seen in western horses that jog abnormally slow.

A trot may also have false extension so that when they reach forward they flip their toe up and the horse hyperextends its forelegs in an exaggerated manner as well. In essence the horse is stretching to cover more ground in the front end but does not provide enough power to push forward. This action is often called "goose-stepping" or "toe-flipping."

## Posting and Diagonals

If you ride English, then you will usually post your trot. This is the up and down movement that makes the trot more comfortable for the English rider. (Actually, the movement is really a forward and back movement where the rider rocks her hips forward and back, using the horse's natural push for the upward movement. But beginner riders are taught up/down simply because it's easier to understand. They will refine the post as they become more experienced.) A sitting trot can be somewhat difficult for English riders and they will usually post; however, dressage riders spend most of their time in the sit trot after warming the horse up in posting trot (to ensure his back is ready for the sitting trot work).

When a horse posts, the rider sits and rises with one diagonal pair of legs. The diagonal is named for the foreleg. For example, if the rider posts with the left front leg and the right hind leg, the rider is posting on the left diagonal. In the United States it is customary for a rider to post on the outside diagonal (except in dressage, when riders will switch their diagonals when asking the horse for more engagement of the hind legs). For example, when riding to the right you are riding on the left diagonal. When the rider changes direction in a turn, they should also switch diagonals. Posting on one diagonal without ever changing puts more stress on those legs and can lead to a horse becoming "one-sided."

Diagonals can be somewhat mysterious to new riders, but if you remember this simple phrase you will always be on the correct diagonal. Now, even though you are going to know this little phrase you do not want to get into the habit of staring at your horse's shoulder to make sure you are on the correct diagonal. Your riding instructor is sure to get onto you for that! Your riding should just feel more natural when you are posting correctly. So, here it is:

### *"Rise and fall with the leg on the wall."*

For example, you are doing a posting trot to the left. Glance down at your horse's shoulder and when you see the horse's right foreleg move forward you will rise in your stirrups. When it moves back you sit. It may take a few strides to get the beat, but once you do you will be on the correct diagonal. Now, when you switch directions it is customary to sit a beat (most riders need to think of the sit a beat as a two-beat—bump, bump-up) and then resume posting. If you can't get back on the correct diagonal then sit through a couple of beats and then rise. That should get you back on track. Riders are usually able to post better going in one direction than in another.

If you switch your diagonals a few times while glancing at the horse's shoulder, you can gradually get the feel of what it is like to post on the correct diagonal. When posting on the wrong one, a rider can often feel that it is a rougher ride. It's usually easier to get the hang of posting if you can consistently practice on the same horse. Since horses' trots vary in rhythm and motion (and bounce), sometimes you, as a beginner, have to re-learn the feel of the correct and incorrect diagonal when riding a different horse.

## The Canter

The canter is three-beat gait with suspension. The canter is like a series of jumps with suspension between strides.

The sequence of the canter is:

- Outside hind leg (First beat)
- Diagonal pair of legs (Second beat)
- Inside foreleg (Third beat)
- Suspension

In the canter, one leg will be leading the motion. This is termed the "lead" that the horse is on.

The sequence for the left lead is:

- Right hind
- Left hind and right fore (Diagonal pair)
- Left fore or leading foreleg (suspension)

The sequence for the right lead is:

- Left hind
- Right hind and left fore (Diagonal pair)
- Right fore or leading foreleg (suspension)

The horse should normally lead with the inside leg. If you are cantering to the left then the horse should be leading with the left fore. If you are cantering to the right then the horse should be leading with the right fore. Cantering with the outside legs leading can make it difficult to turn. This is called a wrong lead or false lead. (In advanced training, especially in hunters and dressage, cantering on the "wrong" lead is called the counter canter, and it is done intentionally as training and supplying movement.)

When a horse changes his leading leg in a turn this is called a "lead change." A horse can change leads in a *flying lead change* by changing within one canter stride. A horse may also do a *simple lead change* by breaking down into the trot for a couple of strides and then change leads when departing back into the canter.

A good canter should be regular, light and active. The canter is more collected than the gallop and the gait has a rocking motion that is easily followed by the seat. The canter is one of the most pleasant gaits for a rider.

The *lope* is a relaxed, unconstrained canter that is performed on a loose rein. The horse remains a three-beat canter with suspension. This horse may have a longer frame and the neck is carried lower and with less suspension. This is typically the western version of the canter.

A good canter requires that a horse remain supple and has good balance and coordination. Some horses may be confused by a cue to canter and take the wrong lead. Other faults include a fumbled canter depart or change of leads because the horse is not balanced in the canter. The term *cross-firing* is when a horse switches leads multiple times when moving in the same direction. The cross-canter should not be confused with cross-firing, as the cross-canter is when a horse is on one lead with his hind legs and the other lead with his forelegs.

## The Gallop

The gallop is a four-beat gait with suspension. The gait is also a series of "jumps" and is the horse's natural running gait. They will use the gallop when they need to get somewhere fast or when they are very afraid. A rider will very rarely use the gallop. The fastest you will usually get is an extended canter. The sequence of the gallop is similar to that of the canter except that the inside hind leg lands first instead of diagonal pairs landing together.

The sequence of the gallop is:

- Outside hind leg
- Inside hind
- Outside foreleg
- Inside (leading) foreleg (suspension)

The sequence of the left lead gallop is:

- Right hind
- Left hind
- Right fore
- Left fore (leading foreleg) (suspension)

The sequence of the right lead gallop is:

- Left hind
- Right hind
- Left fore
- Right fore (leading foreleg) (suspension)

The gallop is an extended gait with long strides. The horse uses his abdominal muscles to help engage his hind legs for each stride. The head and neck oscillate forward and back to balance the horse. The horse takes a breath with each stride. The speed of the gallop may vary from 18 miles per hour to 45 miles per hour.

The *hand gallop* is a controlled gallop that is executed at about 18 miles per hour. The gait should be well-balanced so that the horse can handle direction changes and changes in terrain. This is often used in jumping and may be requested in the show ring.

There are also faults in the gallop and they tend to be similar to that of the canter. A gallop may be on the wrong lead and disunited. A horse may also scramble in the gallop. This is usually because they are going too fast or turning too tightly. This is often seen in barrel racers and jumpers that are trying to beat a clock.

## Backing

The horse rarely backs up naturally and some are more timid about backing than others. If a horse needs to go back from where he came from, he will usually just try to turn around. In some instances, they may find themselves trapped and will back up. The back is an unnatural movement for a horse, as he must engage his hind legs and move back in a diagonal pattern. The back is a four beat maneuver.

The sequence of a back is:

- Right fore
- Left hind
- Left fore
- Right hind

A horse should turn back calmly and flex at the poll and in the mouth. He should also be willing to move forward at any time. The horse should not drag his feet when backing.

## Transitions & Cues

Transitions occur when you change from one gait to another or from a halt. Horses will make transitions easily and automatically on their own, but when riding we need to prompt them through cues. Some riders will give their horses a little extra encouragement by making a clicking noise for a trot and kissing for a canter. (Again, this is often discouraged by English riding instructors.)

In nature, horses make their transitions gradually. They move from a halt to a walk to a trot and then to the canter. The same is true when they slow down. In riding we often skip a gait. So we may go from a walk to a canter. You can also go from a halt to a trot, but the horse is most likely going to have a few walking steps before he breaks into the trot. Skipping a gait requires that a horse be balanced and supple. For a beginner, it is perfectly natural to use the horse's natural way of transitioning and as you become more comfortable with the different gaits you can begin to learn to skip one.

For a smooth transition, the rider must prepare a horse for the transition. By applying the correct aids and using good timing the rider will be able to remain balanced with the horse and the horse's gait changes. If a rider is off-balance and topples forward or backwards, it will upset the horse and they will not change gaits smoothly. You will have to use your natural feel and balance to "feel" when you are ready to change into a transition.

# Chapter 7: After The Ride

When you are done with your ride for the day, you are first going to have to get off your horse. Then there are several other things that you will need to do before you can pat your pony goodnight. These last few tasks should not be neglected for your horse's sake.

## Dismounting

Dismounting is not as difficult as mounting. There are actually two ways that you may choose to do it as well. Depending on the size of your horse, one may be easier than the other. And here is how to do it both ways:

1. Ensure that your horse is at a complete stop. It is very dangerous to dismount a moving horse and you may spook the horse if you do so.
2. Take your right foot out of the stirrup and either grasp the pommel of your English saddle or the horn of your western saddle with left hand. Remember that you must hold on to the reins for control purposes.
3. Swing your right leg over the horse, but be careful not to kick him and then move your right hand to the cantle of the saddle.
4. Lean against the saddle and kick your left foot out and slide down to the ground
5. Or (for English riders) while you are still in the saddle, remove both feet from the stirrups, lean forward, pressing your hands into the horse's neck and gracefully bring your right leg over your horse's rump and slide down to the ground. (Think of this as almost vaulting off.)
6. It is not recommended to leave your left foot in the stirrup and step down to the ground with the right. If your horse spooks or bolts, you're stuck in the stirrup.

Be certain that you always have hold on to your reins for safety purposes. If you are an English rider you are going to want to run your stirrups up the leathers to keep them from banging on your horse.

## Untacking

Your horse is probably going to be ready to get that bridle off his head, as most are. And this is where you are going to want to start. Prepare your horse by placing his halter around his neck as you did when you were bridling the horse. Remember to unbuckle both the noseband, if you have one, and the throatlatch, if you have one. Then gently remove the crown piece from around the ears. The horse will usually spit the bit right out. Do not pull the bit out if the horse does not want to let go right away. Next, place the halter back on the horse's head.

Now you are going to want to remove the English girth or unhook your western girth. When removing an English girth you will want to be certain to undo the left side first and then the right. If you have a western saddle you will unloop the latigo and then loop and tuck it around the D-ring on the saddle. Go to the right side of the horse and lie the girth over the saddle and hook the stirrup around the saddle horn.

Remove the saddle from the left side of the horse. Lift the saddle and the saddle pad together at the same time. And place the saddle on the saddle rack. Place the saddle pad, wet side up, on top of the saddle to allow it to dry. For an English saddle, you will do the same, as well as place the girth wet side up so that it can dry.

## *Cooling Down*

After a hard ride all horses need at least a ten-minute walk to cool down, depending on temperature and the amount of work. You can do this at the end of your riding session or by hand after untacking. This allows them to cool down, lower their heart rate and respiration rate and relax their muscles. You will want to walk your horse until he is cool to the touch on his chest and not blowing visibly in the flanks. The sweat on his body should also be dried and his breathing should be normal. If it is very hot out, you can give him a sponge bath to help him cool down.

Do not allow the horse to eat or drink until he is completely relaxed. Doing so may cause him to colic.

## Post-Ride Grooming

Your horse is typically pretty clean after a ride, but there are a few things you should do to make him comfortable. If the horse got very sweaty you can remove some of the sweat with a sweat scraper. You can also use your sweat scraper to remove excess water if you sponged the horse down. This helps them to dry more quickly.

You will then also want to pick out his feet again. Remove any clods of dirt or rocks that they may have picked up while you were riding. You will also want to give him a good brush down with your soft brush just to lay the hair back down and remove any dust.

# Chapter 8: Riding Safely & Being Prepared

Throughout your riding you want to be as safe as possible. As you know horses are very large animals and, as humans, we are really no match for their strength. There are several safety precautions that you can take to ensure that your ride is a safe and fun one.

There are also several typical behaviors that you want to be prepared for should they occur unexpectedly. Things like bucking, rearing and running away happen to many riders, even ones who have been riding for many years. The key to staying safe in a situation such as this is to know what to expect and how to deal with it.

## Safe Attire

Safety begins with dressing appropriately for horseback riding. As you become experienced and you realize how important safety is when riding, you will cringe when you see people riding in tennis shoes and shorts. This is simply not safe attire for riding, no matter how hot it is outside.

A western rider will be dressed appropriately in jeans, cowboy boots and a shirt that is not loose and baggy. Shirts, whether they are t-shirts or not, should always be tucked in. When you are riding it is very easy for a baggy shirt to get caught on the saddle horn, trees, fencing and anything else you happen to snag on to. Many western riders tend to not wear a helmet, but they are safe and nobody will make fun of you if you choose to wear one. In fact, may helmet manufacturers are making them more appealing so that they are more western in style with the leather and the conchos. Some helmets also appear to be a cowboy hat, only with a chinstrap. It is highly recommended that you always wear a helmet when riding, regardless of tack. Riders have been thrown from western saddles as easily as from English ones. Ensure that your helmet is ASTM-SEI certified. A bicycle helmet simply will not do as it is not manufactured or tested to the same specifications as the equestrian ASTM-SEI helmet.

If you are riding English, you will be most comfortable in breeches or jodhpurs. Tall boots, either dress or field style, are also the best for riding English. Tall boots and beige breeches are the more formal attire and what you will commonly see in the show ring topped with a ratcatcher blouse (if riding hunt seat) and a hunt seat show jacket. Dressage riders compete in white breeches, dressage coat and stock tie (since you cannot see the blouse, dressage riders can wear almost any shirt in the show ring. For casual riding, however, you can wear jeans (specific riding jeans are made for casual riding or tights) and paddock boots as well. Many riders will also wear breeches and tall boots for casual riding because they are very comfortable. Many English riders will often choose to wear schooling chaps or half-chaps if they do choose to wear jeans. Shirts should always be tucked and close fitting.

All clothing should be based on the weather. If it's cold, then you are going to want to bundle up. Wear gloves, a coat and sweaters. You may also want to wear socks that are extra thick. If it's warm then feel free to where t-shirts, tank tops and other close fitting items that will keep you cool, but safe at the same time.

# Helmets

You should always wear an ASTM-SEI certified helmet when riding. Be careful when purchasing English type helmets because there are several that are for dress only and not certified for safety. Helmets come in a variety of styles. In the picture you see a helmet that has been designed for winter riding because it keeps your ears warm. Certification means that they have been designed to improve impact absorption and to have increased strength. The helmet should be properly fitted with a harness or chin strap. If you have already been thrown from a horse with a helmet on, then it is most likely not as strong as it should be. Most helmet companies will replace your helmet free of charge if this has happened. Also, please make certain that the helmet is designed for equestrians. Please do not show up at the barn with a bike helmet on! It will not provide the protection you need.

There are also special vests that you may consider if you are going to be jumping. Children should definitely wear them if they are jumping. They are thin and will fit beneath your riding shirt. These vests offer a degree of protection against rib cage, collar bone and spinal injuries.

## What You Should Never Wear When Riding

Everyday people get hurt because they wear the wrong attire when riding horses. Here is a list of things you should never wear when riding a horse.

- Tennis shoes
- Sandals
- Shorts
- Oversized shirts
- Open-toed shoes
- Shoes with no heels
- Slip on shoes
- Baggy pants

You may also want to be sure that you don't wear very nice clothing when riding. Your favorite jeans or your favorite shirt is sure to get dirty with some stains that don't come out. In fact, you will probably have a collection of t-shirts with permanent, big, brown horse kisses on the shoulder or back.

## Spooking

All horses will spook while you are on board at some point in time. How dramatic it will be shall depend largely on how you react to his reaction. Because horses are prey animals they are always on the alert, just about anything that comes from out of nowhere will spook them easily. (Old trusted school horses are usually desensitized to most noises or scary things, so many of them are what instructors might call "bombproof."

Usually a horse that spooks will shy away at something and simply sidestep or hop to the side a bit. Others will spook and run away from whatever has scared them.

If the spook is very dramatic, it is very easy for a rider to become unseated. If your horse spooks for some reason, then you are going to want to remain calm and hold your balance. You can usually feel a horse is going to spook because his whole body becomes tense. Allow the horse to turn and face whatever is scaring him. This is often enough to calm him down. If the horse refuses to pass the object, you may need to get off and walk him by it. Horses are often much more brave when they are led by something rather than being ridden.

Some horses use a spook as an evasive maneuver when they are used to having their riders dismount when they've spooked before. (Dismounting can be almost a reward to a horse that is spooking.) To ride through a spook and push the horse past the scary object, try the following: put both calves on him with a constant squeeze. Applying calf pressure often calms a nervous horse. Then ride shoulder fore, with the horse bent slightly away from the object. Maintain calf pressure. For example, if the horse refuses to pass a big tarp on the right, bend him slightly to the left by squeezing your left rein and applying your left leg. Use your seat to drive him forward by pushing with the following seat. Think of pushing a book across a table with your hips. Keep squeezing with your calves and driving with your seat while maintaining the shoulder fore past the object.

## Bucking

Bucking is usually due to a horse that has too much energy. Or, they may have learned that the quickest way to end a ride is to buck the rider off. Some horses will often buck if they are in pain. This is usually due to an ill-fitting saddle and often kidney problems. If you change saddles and you know it is not due to training issues, it is often wise to have a veterinarian examine the horse.

If a horse bucks frequently when you are riding, you may want to begin each ride with a longeing warm-up. However, remember that this does not teach the horse that he shouldn't buck while you are aboard. It will just allow the horse to get out any excess energy, without you being on board. You may also need to check and see if the saddle is pinching the horse.

If you horse does buck you off and you are not seriously injured, then you need to get back on the horse. This shows the horse that bucking is not an easy way for him to end the ride. If you can't get back on by yourself, then have someone else ride him for you. It is best if you get on so you do not develop any fears about being bucked off as well.

To get a real good buck, a horse needs to drop his head so that he can lift his hindquarters high. If you keep your horse from dropping his head down, he will not be able to get the leverage to give a strong buck. Also, if you apply your leg and drive him forward, he will be more inclined to give you a rolling buck rather than a real bucking bronco buck. So, keep your back strong and don't allow him to pull the reins from your hands then use your legs to drive him forward.

Using discipline, like cracking him on the butt with a crop while he bucks will also help a horse to understand that bucking will not be tolerated.

## Rearing

Rearing is one of the most dangerous bad habits a horse can have. This is when the horse stands on his hind legs and lifts his front feet off the ground. Many old horsemen will tell you that the front feet are more dangerous than the hind. Some horses rear at things approaching them in the front or when a severe bit is being used on them. Bits can cause rearing because the pain is in their mouths and the only way they know how to get away from it is to go up.

Rearing while being ridden is a dangerous habit that should not be tolerated. If a horse rears when you ask him to do something that he doesn't want to do you need to wait it out and shift your weight forward. Shifting your weight backward or pulling on the reins will cause the horse to fall over backwards onto you.

With a rearing horse, you must seek professional help. However, if you find yourself on a horse that is rearing, try to keep him moving forward with your seat and leg. By using a rein to turn him, you can set him off balance so he cannot rear. When you can, dismount a horse that has reared. You should also not ride the horse until a trainer has fixed this problem. Rearing horses are not for beginners.

## Running Away

Most well trained horses will never run away, but in some instances there is something that is scary enough to frighten them that badly. For example, if a pack of dogs flushes out of the woods and spooks your horse while you are in a trail ride. If one horse begins to run, most of the others will follow. If you ever lose control in this situation, do your best to ride it out. When you feel that you can begin to try and control the horse you will use the pulley rein and a calm "whoa". The pulley rein should make the horse turn into a circle. Work the horse into a smaller and smaller circle.

## Backing without Being Asked

Very few horses will do this because they do not usually like to go backward. The horse is usually trying to resist you when he does that. First of all you want to make sure that you are not accidentally telling the horse to go backward. If you are not and the horse is just trying to get out of work, then you want to make him work.

Make the horse go backward until he doesn't want to do that anymore. When he doesn't want to do that, keep making him go backward. Then, **after you decide** to go forward, cue the horse to go forward. You will often find that this is an easy way to fix this problem. You may spend a whole day backing, but he will learn that he is going to have to work one way or another.

Backing up is sometimes a precursor evasion behavior that, if not fixed, can turn into rearing. When a horse feels like he is running backward, use a driving seat to push him forward and close your calves on his sides.

Some western horses are trained to back when the rider leans forward. This can be confusing when an English hunt seat rider tries to ride the same horse because the hunt seat rider often inclines her upper body forward to ask a horse to move on. The western horse can take this as the cue to back. If you are riding a western-trained horse and he starts to back up without you asking, check your body position and ensure that you sit up straight. Lean back slightly even to see if he stops. If he does, the backing may just have been a miscommunication.

# Chapter 9: Exercise and Training Routines

If you're a new rider, one of your primary goals when riding is getting your horse used to you (listening to you) and getting used to your horse (listening to him). When you're riding, it's important that you keep your horse ready for the next command and not looking around and trying to find something else to be interested in. You can do this when you ride by changing up the routine frequently and you can apply suppling exercises that make your horse suppler and less stiff, almost like stretching for people.

How do you do this? Don't just wander aimlessly around the arena, walking lap after lap, and then doing the same thing at the trot, without incorporating changes in the routine to keep him fresh and listening. There are several ways you can practice this while riding—one way is by riding gait transitions and the other way is by riding patterns.

Start with gait transitions. Begin at the walk because your horse will need time to warm up. (You wouldn't go out and start jogging yourself without a warm up, would you?) While walking, get the feel of how sensitive your horse is by asking him to halt every couple of strides. To ask him to halt, sit very deep in the saddle so he slows by feeling your weight and gently bring the reins back toward your belly. As soon as he halts, immediately give with your hands forward so you don't punish him for doing something right.

While riding, practicing gait transitions is a simple way for you and your horse to get the feel for each other. Gait transitions are when you change your gait, for example, going from walk to trot/jog or lope/canter to walk. By asking your horse to routinely change gaits every few strides, you'll keep him sensitive and looking for you as he's ready for the next command. Practice gait transitions from walk to halt, halt to walk, walk to trot/jog, trot/jog to walk, walk to halt, halt to rein back, rein back to halt, halt to walk, walk to trot/jog, trot/jog to canter/lope, etc. Apply the gait transitions as you see fit to your level. For example, if you're not ready to canter/lope, then wait until you have better control and balance.

Now we can ride one of the most simple of the patterns—a circle. When you're ready to walk off, apply your calves in a squeeze of his sides. Get a forward marching walk so your horse is using himself. Walk a few strides and turn him in a big (20 meter) circle. Give him a little squeeze as you begin to turn him because many horses slow down as they are being turned into a circle. Circling helps get your horse to supple and get more limber while you're warming him up. Circling also keeps you to get the horse's attention. Circle once and continue the way you were going.

Your circle should be nicely round, like a real circle. Your horse should be on the arc of the circle, with his body bent in the same arc. To ride a circle, use your inside leg behind the girth to push his rib cage and round his backbone. You can also lightly squeeze your inside rein to get his nose turned slightly inside. If you turn your head and look toward the center of the circle, you can see in your peripheral vision both the corner of his eye and the point of his croup or hip. Then you know you have a nice bend through your horse's back.

Now that you know how to circle, you can build on this figure by incorporating other figures into your routine:

**Spirals**: while walking on the circle, get your horse to expand the size of the circle by picturing the circle with multiple rings that become tracks. You will be riding your horse on different imaginary tracks. To ride your horse to the outer track, sit into your outside stirrup by weighting your outside seat bone, lightly push your horse on and off with your inside leg. You'll feel him step over. Now hold him to that imaginary track by blocking further movement to the outer rings with your outside leg and moving your weight to be centered in the saddle. Now take your horse to an inner ring by sitting into your inside stirrup, weighting your inside seat bone and pushing with your outside leg. Hold him to the inner track by blocking further movement with your inside leg and sitting square in the saddle.

**Figure 8**: walk a big circle, and as you are finishing the circle and are coming back to where you began it, prepare to go the other way and form another circle in the other direction immediately next to the first circle. Keep both circles the same size and shape. Apply your bending aids that you learned from riding circles and spirals so that each circle on the figure 8 is nicely round. As you come across the center and are about to change direction, ride your horse straight for two strides, then change the bend. You can also incorporate gait transitions by halting at the center between the two circles once you've completed the figure 8.

**Serpentine**: a serpentine is made up of big loops where you ask your horse to change direction across the arena each time you reach the rail. Serpentines can be made up of three or four equal loops. To ride a serpentine, for example, as you turn from the short side down the long side of an arena, go across the center of the arena, ride straight directly across the other long side and change direction going down the long side. Ride a few more strides, look across the arena and ride across the center again now toward the other long side. As you get to the side, change direction again and ride a few more strides, look across to the other long side, turn through the center of the arena and head to the other long side, switching direction when you get to it. Important concepts to keep in mind when riding a serpentine are: 1) Keeping the horse balanced and not falling in at each turn (do so by sitting square in the saddle but weighting the seat bone for the direction you wish to turn to. Apply your bending aids each time you turn. 2) Ride the straight across the arena parts of the serpentine absolutely as straight as you can. As you turn, find a spot on the wall or arena to ride to that is straight across from you and ride straight to it using your leg and seat aids.

**Simple serpentine**: a simple serpentine is ridden from the long side rail to the quarter line of the arena. As you come out of the turn from the short side to the long side, begin riding your horse on a diagonal with a bend toward the inside to the quarter line. When you reach the quarter line straighten the horse for one stride and then change the bend so that he bends toward the rail and ride him on a diagonal back to the rail. Straighten him for a stride, then change the bend toward the inside and ride him to the quarter line and repeat. This is an exercise in changing your horse's bend and will make him supple nicely.

**Leg yield** (side pass in western): a leg yield is a figure in which the horse responds to your seat and leg aid to move forward and across (crossing his legs over each other). In English riding, a leg yield is called a lateral movement because the horse moves laterally. To ride a leg yield, as you are coming down through the short side of the arena heading toward the long side, turn early so that you are on the arena's quarter line (figure at least 5 feet from the arena wall). Ride the quarter line straight, then step into your outside stirrup (the stirrup toward the wall) and apply your inside leg in an on off command. On off. On Off. On off. You should feel your horse step over, across and forward. Ride the leg yield to the rail.

**Volte and reverse**: to ride a volte and reverse is like riding a tear drop shape. You head down the long side and begin turning in like turning into a small circle, but instead ride back to the rail, now going the other way. Remember to keep the loop round and leg yield back to the rail.

All of these pattern exercises will help you and your horse no only to listen to each other but will also help you learn how to ride him straight, through transitions and achieving the correct bend to keep his back and hindquarters supple. Doing this work also helps you to develop both your balance and coordination. An added plus to riding gait transitions and lateral movements is that they strengthen the horse, particularly in the hindquarters and hind legs. Also, riding such patterns helps calm the horses that are anxious or worried about their environments. You're giving them a job to think about while also asking them to work and use their bodies correctly.

Now that you've got this down at the walk, it's time to try it at the trot/jog. Then you can incorporate gait transitions within the patterns.

When you're riding your horse in gait transitions or in patterns, or any particular exercise, it's important to remember how sensitive he is even if you don't think he is particularly sensitive to your riding aids (legs, hands and seat) at all. Think of how reactive he is to the presence of an annoying fly buzzing at his legs and belly. He swishes his tail, kicks up a leg and tries rubbing off the fly from his belly.

Being sensitive makes sense for horses because in the wild if they were not sensitive to their surroundings, they would likely be another animal's prey.

Now let's take the horse out of his natural environment and have him live with humans. Put him with a human who repeatedly exposed him to conflicting aids. An example of conflicting aids would be kicking his sides and pulling the reins at the same time or not being able to control a leg bouncing at the horse's sides. When horses are faced with this kind of stimuli they eventually shut down their awareness of that area, becoming deadened or dulled in that area. So, the horse begins to tune out the aids and is more difficult to get moving, requiring much kicking and clucking, even a few taps with the whip. This horse has become desensitized to the leg. To keep your horse from becoming desensitized, it's important for you to work hard on keeping your riding aids distinctive and steady.

Desensitization can also occur when riders don't give their horses sufficient rewards for doing things right when being ridden. The term "reward" doesn't mean carrots or horse treats and kindly pats on the neck. The best reward you can give your horse is an end to his work for the day. By ending your horse's work, you've told him he's done well and you've rewarded him for that.

A horse that is made to do an exercise over and over, even when he does it well, eventually becomes desensitized and may then grow sour. Why shouldn't he? He's trying to please you but you keep making him do the same thing over and over, so he doesn't know when he's done it correctly. When riding your horse, you are always training him, even if you are a new rider with little experience. You're telling your horse what he must do when you ask him and what he cannot do, so no matter how inexperienced you are, your horse is still going to learn from you—the good and the bad that you may be teaching him.

# Chapter 10: Horse Breeds and Markings

Hundreds of horse breeds can be found throughout the world. Each breed has unique characteristics that were bred for particular uses. Though you can find most of them in the U.S., more common are several traditionally popular horse breeds in the United States. Because some disciplines are more popular in some areas of the country than in others, some breeds are more common in some areas than others. Here, we will talk about the most popular breeds that you will find in the U.S. where different riding disciplines are more popular than others.

When you are considering buying a horse, you might be interested in owning one of the popular breeds. If you are interested in showing and competing in breed-specific shows or breeding your horse, then you may want to look at your options with these breeds as far as registered horses and registries go. Many of these horse breeds possess qualities that horse owners and breeders have grown to love.

Many people successfully show and compete with horses that do not have a known breed pedigree. If you don't have interest in competing in breed-specific shows, you will find your options are wide.

You should also remember that there are other competition options available to you if you do not find a registered horse. The United States Dressage Federation, United States Equestrian Federation, National Cutting Horse Association and National Reining Horse Association do not require that horses be registered by breed. You also have the option of rodeo and similar activities. Hunter/jumper, dressage and event competitions allow riders to show their horses regardless of breed and registration. There are several crossbreeds and grade horses based off of the popular breeds as well as crossbreeds of other interesting types that make excellent competitors or weekend companions.

It is also important to realize that although many horses in these breeds will have similar personality characteristics, each horse is a unique individual just as you are a unique individual. Their upbringing from foalhood shapes them just as your upbringing from childhood shapes you. For example, Shetland ponies are renowned for their grumpy and stubborn attitudes, but there are those Shetland ponies that are adorable and loveable as well. Arabians are also known for being high-strung, but there are those that make excellent mounts and are extremely trustworthy.

That being said, let's move on to some of the traditionally popular horse breeds in the U.S.

## Appaloosa

The Appaloosa is an American breed that has descended from the Spanish Jennet. The Spanish Jennet was brought to the Americas by Spanish conquistadors in the 15<sup>th</sup> century. This is one of the most popular breeds in the United States and they are found in numerous events. They are compact horses with strong, athletic ability.

**Colors:** Five Basic Coat patterns – Blanket, Marble, Leopard, Snowflake and Frost. No grays or pintos are registered.

**Height:** 14.2 – 16 hands

**Recommended Events:** Endurance, Trail riding, Western stock horse classes, Jumping, Dressage, Good family horse

# Arabian

The Bedouin tribes of the Arabian Peninsula established the Arabian approximately 18 centuries ago. The Arabian was bred for desert life and for guerrilla warfare. In the 1980s there were many hot-blooded horses bred in a way that they were difficult to handle. These horses were bred for show purposes, but many became dangerous. The breed has settled back into an all-around breed that enjoys a variety of different events.

**Colors:** Grey, Chestnut, Bay, Roan, and Black
**Height:** 14.2 – 15.1 hands

**Recommended Events:** Endurance, Dressage, Jumping, and Driving

# Miniature

You might not be able to ride these little guys, but they are one of the most popular breeds and they are very versatile. These are small horses, not ponies that have been stunted in growth by the harsh environments that the horse developed in. These included scarce food sources, rough terrain and severe weather. The horses were used in the U.S. to pull carts through the tunnels of coalmines. The first true minis were developed in Europe in the 17th century and bred as pets for nobility. Miniature horses have exactly the same conformation as a full-size horse.

**Colors:** All horse colors

**Height:** There are two height divisions in the American Miniature Horse Association:

- **A Division:** 34 inches and under
- **B Division:** 34 inches up to 38 inches

**Recommended Events:** Pleasure driving, Halter, Specialty events developed for their size, Companions

# Morgan

The story of the Morgan begins in 1790 with a schoolteacher named Justin Morgan of Randolph, Vermont. He was given a yearling colt name Figure as a repayment for a debt. The colt became a beautiful stallion and was in high demand as a stud. Today, nearly all the Morgans are traced back to him. The stud also made several contributions to many of the other breeds in the Americas. The horse is very versatile and diverse.

**Colors:** Bay, Black, Brown, Chestnut, Grey, Palomino, Cream, Dun, Buckskin

**Height:** 14.1-15.2 hands

**Recommended Events:** Driving, Jumping, Dressage, Cattle Cutting, Cross-Country Endurance, Therapeutic Riding, Good for Children.

# Paint Horse

Paints are often mistakenly called pintos. It is important to understand the difference between these colored horses. The Paint Horse is actually a breed while the pinto is a color. So, many Paints are pintos, but not all pintos are paints. The Paint is actually the result of many Quarter Horse crossings. These are stock type horses that cannot be registered with the American Quarter Horse Association because of their white markings, despite the fact that many of these horses are predominantly Quarter Horse bred. In the 1960s the breed itself developed when a group of Paint Horse enthusiasts began breeding and promoting the horses as an individual breed. There are three coat markings in the breed including:

- **Tobiano:** This horse is a white base with dark patches of color on top.
- **Overo:** These horses are predominantly a dark colored base with white markings on top. These markings are almost jagged appearing on some horses.
- **Tovero:** This is a horse that combines both of the marking categories. They have characteristics of both tobianos and overos.

**Colors:** Various colors are seen within the marking classifications including Black, Bay, Brown, Chestnut, Palomino, Grey, Roan, Sorrel, and Buckskin.

**Height:** 15-16 hands

**Recommended Events:** Western stock classes, Ranch Work, Trail Riding, English Classes, Driving, Jumping, Dressage, Pleasure Horses, Flat Racing

## Quarter Horse

The American Quarter Horse is now the most popular breed in the world. The American Quarter Horse Association has affiliate registries in various countries and the number of registered horses has reached 4 million. The breed is very versatile and competes in Western, English and Pleasure Driving. The breed is also becoming a popular dressage horse.

**Colors:** All colors, except pinto. There are rules on how much white the horse may have and where it may extend to on the horse.

**Height:** 14-16 hands

**Recommended Events:** All Western, English, Jumping, Dressage, Driving, Ranch Work, Trail Riding, Flat Racing, and Pleasure horse

# Saddlebred

The Saddlebred is a gaited horse that has been developed from several breeds such as the Morgan, the Narragansett Pacers and Spanish horses. The horse was developed in Kentucky as a mount that could carry a rider comfortably over long distances. The horse has a famous four beat gait known as the *rack*, a *stepping pace*, in addition to the walk, trot and canter, all of which are very animated. There are five-gait and three-gait Saddlebreds. The five-gait horses can perform the three basic gaits plus the rack and the stepping pace. The three-gait horses perform only the three basic gaits. The Saddlebred tends to carry its head rather high and moves in a collected manner. The body is lean. These horses are often ridden saddle seat or are driven. Some may be ridden English or western.

**Colors:** Bay, Black, Brown, Chestnut, Sorrel, and Grey. Some may also be pintos.
**Height:** 15-17 hands
**Recommended Events:** Saddleseat classes, such as English Pleasure and Driving. Some have excelled in dressage and even jumping.

## Standardbred

Standardbreds are commonly used in harness racing, although many have made excellent riding companions. These horses originated early in American history and were developed specifically for harness racing. The Standardbred may perform at either a trot or a pace. The horse is born with the innate ability to move at the trot or pace with great speed. Some have been known to trot at nearly 30 miles per hour. The pace is easily recognized as the horse's legs move in unison on one side of the body. These horses are closely related to the Thoroughbred and after their racing careers have ended they can be seen at horse shows competing in both English and western events. Some have been successful in dressage.

**Colors:** Bay, Brown, Black, Chestnut and Grey.
**Height:** 15 to 16 hands
**Recommended Events:** Harness Racing, English classes, Western Classes, Pleasure mounts

## Tennessee Walking Horse

The Tennessee Walking Horse was developed in the 18th century. They were also desirable for their ability to cover a large amount of ground at a relatively comfortable pace. These horses were popular on plantations as they could carry the rider long distances as well as pull a cart to take the family to town. The Tennessee Walker, as they are often called, is a gaited horse that performs the three basic gaits plus the their famous four-beat running walk. These horses have a relatively straight head and larger ears. They have prominent withers and a graceful neck.

**Colors:** All solid colors and pinto.

**Height:** 15 to 16 hands

**Recommended Events:** Saddleseat classes, English classes, Western classes, Trail Riding

## Thoroughbred

Considered the world's fastest horse, the horse is often considered the most elegant as well. The breed has tremendous energy and determination. These horses have huge potential in all equestrian events. The Thoroughbred was developed in Europe during the 1700s for racing where their breeding began with three foundation sires—the Godolphin Arabian, the Darley Arabian and the Byerly Turk. The breed has influenced several breeds such as the Quarter Horse, Paint and Standardbred.

**Colors:** Most solid colors, roans are rare
**Height:** 14.2-18 hands
**Recommended Events:** Racing, Show Jumping, Cross-Country, Eventing, Hunting, Dressage, and Polo

Baroque breeds are becoming increasingly popular. They are centuries old breeds that were bred as war horses. The term "baroque" refers to the style of art of that era. Examples of the baroque horses are the Lipizzaner, Andalusian and Lusitano. Because they were compactly built for war, with the ability to sit dramatically in their hindquarters with light front ends, these horses are commonly found performing dressage.

## *Popular Pony Breeds*

Ponies are small horses that stand shorter than 14.2 hands. Ponies are distinctive and not all small horses are considered ponies. There are several popular pony breeds and some may be ridden by adults, not just by children. Because ponies are very popular as first horses for children, it is important to cover the popular breeds.

## Shetland

The Shetland is the epitome of ponies. They are often the pony that pops into your head when you hear the word. This breed is actually one of the smaller ponies and is excellent for children when they are properly trained. They do tend to have reputation for stubbornness, but this is not true for all of them.

**Colors:** Most solid colors and pintos
**Height:** 11 hands
**Recommended Events:** English or western events, driving

# Welsh

The Welsh is larger than the Shetland and come in four varieties including the Welsh Cob, Welsh Mountain Pony, Welsh Pony of Cob Type and Welsh Pony. They are droughty breeds and popular with farmers. They are excellent in therapy programs and at crossing treacherous terrain. The different varieties differ in height and some are suitable for adults.

**Colors:** Black, Grey, Bay, and Chestnut
**Height:** 13.2-16 hands
**Recommended Events:** Trekking, Trail Riding, Hunting, Driving, and a Child's Second Pony

# Connemara

The Connemara is a refined pony with some Thoroughbred and Arabian type traits. The pony is somewhat on the tall side and they excel in jumping events. Some are suitable for adults and all are suitable for children. The Connemara is Ireland's only indigenous pony. The ancestors of this pony are believed to have been similar to the Shetland, the Norwegian Ford and the Celtic Pony. Spanish horses have also influenced the breed.

**Colors: Bay, Grey, Black, Dun, Brown**
**Height:** 13-14.2 hands
**Recommended Events:** English classes, Jumping, Cross-Country, Eventing, Dressage, Driving

# Pony of the Americas

The Pony of the Americas or POA is a cross between the Shetland and the Appaloosa. These ponies often have typical Appaloosa markings. The pony is very popular among children and some adults. They make excellent mounts and the American POA Association features an extensive youth horse show program.

**Colors:** Typical Appaloosa colors and markings
**Height:** 11.2 to 14 hands
**Recommended Events:** Western and English classes

## Warmbloods

With English events such as jumping, dressage and cross-country becoming more popular, the interest in European Warmbloods is also on the rise. There are several Warmblood horses and many have similar characteristics. The terms of "hot-blooded," "Warmblooded" and "cold-blooded" refer to the temperament of the horses. The cold-blooded horses are often considered more docile and heavy. These horses are typically draught breeds. Thoroughbreds, Akhal-Teke and Andalusians are considered hot-blooded. Most Warmbloods are the result of crossing Thoroughbreds or light riding horses with draught breeds that were being used as carriage horses (so they were a little more refined than draft horses pulling plows). Germany has produced a large number of the Warmblood breeds and possibly more than any other country, but Warmbloods have also been bred in other countries. If you're interested in a Warmblood, you can find Irish Sporthorses, Swedish Warmbloods, Dutch Warmbloods, Russian Warmbloods, and Holsteiners, among others in addition to the ones described below. These breeds have excelled at Dressage, Driving, Show Jumping, Hunters, Cross-Country and numerous other equestrian events.

# Hanoverian

This breed is a popular Warmblood breed that is one of the most prominent riding horses. The breed was the inspiration of King George II of England, who directed the Celle stud in Lower Saxony to produce a coach horse that would also be suitable for agriculture in 1735. The horse was then developed into a military mount. The modern Hanoverian is very powerful with big, springy movements. They are also known to be level-headed and calm.

**Colors:** Chestnut was predominate, but other colors are available
**Height:** 15.3-17.2 hands
**Recommended Events:** Dressage, Show Jumping, Cross-Country, and Eventing

## Trakehner

The Trakehner began in 1732, when Friedrich Wilhelm I of Prussia gathered his finest horses at the Trakehn stud. The goal was to breed a light cavalry horse. By 1940, there were approximately 80,000 Trakehners in existence and many had won Olympic gold medals. They also had numerous steeplechase records. In 1945, Prussia was invaded and many of the horses died. Through various evacuation attempts, about 1000 of the horses managed to reach the safety of Western Germany. They have undergone rigorous testing and evaluations to be entered into the studbook and the resulting horse has been a free-moving animal that is balanced and elegant.

**Colors:** Chestnut, Gray, Bay, and Black
**Height:** 15.3-17 hands
**Recommended Events:** Dressage, Endurance, Not recommended for beginners

# Oldenburg

The Oldenburg was developed by Count Anton von Oldenburg in the 17th century. The horse was large, black and a proud carriage horse. Today, the horses are very popular mounts in world-class equestrian events.

**Colors:** Black, Dark Bay
**Height:** 16.1-17.3 hands
**Recommended Events:** Show Jumping, Dressage, Eventing, and Driving

## Westphalian

The Westphalian is the second most popular German Warmblood next to the Hanoverian. The stallions have undergone a variety of tests and assessments before being entered in the studbook. They have won numerous Olympic medals in dressage and eventing.

**Colors:** All solid colors
**Height:** 15.2-17.2 hands
**Recommended Events:** Dressage, Show Jumping, and Eventing

## Colors and Markings

The best way to understand the different colors of horses is to see them first hand. It is important to realize that each color will vary in shade somewhat depending on the horse. The colors can also change in the sun, for example, a black horse will have a brownish tinge if they are left out to pasture in the sun.

## White or Cremellos

Whites are often really albinos or cremellos. There has always been a saying that goes, "All white horses are grey horses." It is true that most whitish horses are actually grey horses, but there are also albinos and cremellos. These horses are solid white with pink muzzles. The horses have light colored hooves and may have blue or brown eyes.

# Grey

Grey horses are available in different shades. These horses may be nearly white or dark and dappled. The white hairs mix with a dark hair of any dark color to produce the grey appearance. Foals are often born as solid colors such as charcoal or brown and they lighten, as they grow older. Grey horses have black skin, unlike white horses. Grey is actually not a true color. In horse color genetics, grey horses carry a particular gene that masks their true color. The Lipizzaner breed (often called the "dancing white horses of Austria) is traditionally always grey, though a very rare bay or black may be born every now and then.

## Pinto

Pinto markings are similar to that of Paint markings. Pinto markings usually consist of patches of dark against white, or *overo*. Only certain breeds will display pinto markings.

# Grulla

Grulla horses are characterized by having a smoky brown appearance. They feature a black mane and tail and often black legs. They also have a stripe down their back called a *dorsal stripe*. They may be mistaken as dark buckskins.

## Buckskin

The buckskin will be of yellow or goldish body color. Their mane and tails are black. They will also have black legs. True buckskins do not have a dorsal stripe, although many horses that are characterized as buckskins do.

## Palomino

Palominos feature a golden, yellow body color with flaxen white mane and tails.

## Dun

The dun color is considered to be one of the closest colors to that of the "wild" horse color. This is due to the dorsal stripe and striping that appears on the lower legs of these horses.

## Red Duns

Red duns are duns with a reddish hint to their coat. They have the dorsal stripe running down their backs and may have a flaxen mane and tail. Some red duns will have the same red colored mane and tail as well.

## Chestnut

Chestnuts have a distinct red color to their bodies with the same colored mane and tails. There are various shades of chestnut ranging from light to a dark liver color.

## Sorrel

Sorrels and chestnuts are often used interchangeably. The main difference between chestnut and sorrel is that they have a yellowish tint to their body. Their mane and tail may be of the same body color or flaxen.

## Bay

The bay is a dark brown to reddish brown body. Their mane and tail is always black and they always have black on the lower parts of their legs. The amount of black on the legs may vary.

## Brown

Brown horses will have brown body coloration and brown legs. They should also have a brown muzzle, flank and upper legs. There may be some black on the lower legs and the mane and tail is often black.

# Roan

Roans come in variety of shades. There are red roans, strawberry roans, and blue roans. These horses will have a uniform mixture of white and red hairs or white and black hairs. They often have a black or brown head with black legs. The mane and tail may be black or chestnut.

## Black

A horse that is truly black must be solid black with no white anywhere on his body. The mane and tail must be black as well.

## *Markings*

Each horse will often have distinguishable markings. These markings can be considered somewhat of a fingerprint for horses, as there are no two horses that have identical markings. These markings are often used to distinguish two horses. Each marking has a name and they are used among all equine professionals from trainers to veterinarians. Each marking may have a subtle variation and not be "textbook" as each horse is genetically different.

# Face Markings

**Bald:** A bald face horse has white that begins above the forehead and down to the muzzle. The white will also extend beyond the bridge of their nose and onto the side of the face.

**Blaze:** A blaze is a white area that runs down along the bridge of the nose. They are often a wide, white stripe.

**Snip:** A snip is a little spot of white that is located on the muzzle above the lip.

**Star:** A star is a white spot on the forehead.

**Stripe:** A narrow white stripe down the center of the face. These are much thinner than a blaze, although they are in the same area.

Many horses will have a combination of disjointed facial markings such as a star, stripe and snip.

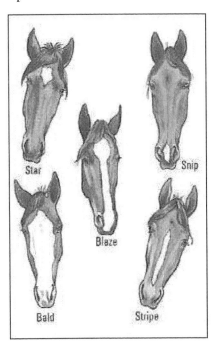

# Leg Markings

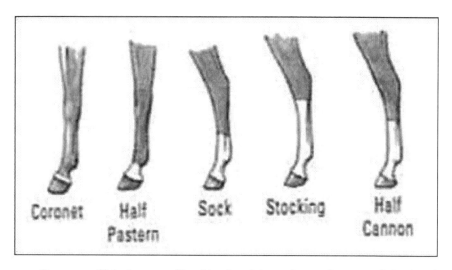

**Coronet:** This is a small white band just above the top of the hoof, where the coronet is located.

**Half Cannon:** White on the leg that extends halfway up the middle of the cannon bone, they are longer than a sock, but shorter than a stocking.

**Half Pastern:** A half pastern is white that extends halfway up the pastern.

**Sock:** White that extends two-thirds of the way up the cannon of the leg.

**Stocking:** White that extends from the hoof up to the knee or the hock.

# Chapter 11: Conclusion

Now you have a basic understanding of the horse, how to prepare for riding and how to start riding. I hope you enjoyed this book. If you would like more advanced information on horse training and riding, please visit www.HorseTrainingResources.com.

A wise horse trainer once said that there's never a never or always when it comes to horses. She meant that each horse, rider and situation bring their own uniqueness. However, there is one always—always set yourself up for a safe ride. If you follow the safety recommendations made in this book, you'll have the tools for a successful and safe ride. Happy trails!

Made in the USA
Las Vegas, NV
14 December 2022

61762017R10076